Joy In The Journey

1ˢᵗ year chronicles from a stay-at-home dad

*Keep chasing your dreams.
Make sure you leave a
little room to enjoy the
joy in the journey.*

"Jo"

By
Jonathan Oliver

Contents

Lesson 1

A New Frontier

"We're having a baby!!!"

Those were the words that my wife said to me 10 months ago. Now, I'm en route to becoming a dad any day now. When I first heard those words, "I'm pregnant", my life flashed before my eyes. I began to question my-self—*Am I going to be a good dad?* Fear began to take over my mind—*I hope I don't mess this up, I can't repeat the sins of my father, What do I need to know about becoming a dad? I must be somewhat qualified given my life experience. I'm a life coach, a professional speaker, a writer, and a former college athlete. That should count for something right?! How can I make sure that I become the best dad I can possibly be with the same tenacity I used in other areas of my life?*

I needed to lean into this new frontier, so the first thing I did was watch pregnancy videos on YouTube—that wasn't my best decision. The second thing I decided to do was make an appointment with my therapist. He shared with me some of the best advice I had gotten thus far: my biggest struggle can become my biggest asset as a parent. Then while doing a little research, I discovered a little nugget that sealed the deal for me. Don't worry about being a great dad. Being a great dad isn't about holding the baby just right, or knowing how to burp her, or being a willing participant at an imaginary tea party. Being a good dad starts with being a good husband. It starts with getting involved in the entire prenatal process and embracing that experience with your wife. So if you really want to be a good dad, make darn sure you're a good husband, because great husbands become great dads.

If there's one thing your baby needs, it's a stable, loving home. Work to make your marriage rock solid. The good dad thing will follow, guaranteed. Once I understood this, I slowly felt the pressure ease from my shoulders.

My wife and I have been married for six years and are closer now than ever before. We communicate better, we speak about our fears, doubts, and worries, we laugh and celebrate each other's success. We have been broken and healed together in a way only God can do. More importantly, we pray together daily. So I am going to embrace this new frontier going in with eyes wide open as well as with an open mind. I'm going to soak up this new and exciting adventure and share my joy in the journey along the way.

Lesson 2

The Waiting Game

The due date for our daughter, Journey has come and passed, and she has yet to grace us with her presence. I admit that I am impatient, and I know patience is a virtue but at this moment, Journey is teaching me that she has her own plans, however, I am guilty of wanting to exercise patience on *my* own terms. Maybe I'm the only person who has prayed and asked God for patience, and when God places it at my feet, I then pray to speed up the process as quickly as possible. Maybe that's just me ...... but I doubt that.

With regards to hastening the delivery of our daughter, patience on my terms means supporting my wife with: long walks, sex (for induction purposes...not complaining), labor inducing massages, acupuncture pressure points, eating spicy foods, and finally her drinking castor oil followed by a shot of orange juice—apparently that's a thing. I think later on this month when there's a full moon or eclipse or something lunar, that's supposed to help bring Journey forth as well—I was wrong. In terms of God's patience, Journey will be here when she gets here and not a moment too late.

Recently, I've been in the process of reading two really good books that are helping me better understand this waiting game. The first is *Shepherding a Child's Heart* by Tedd Tripp, which teaches you what your goals as a parent ought to be and how to practically pursue those ends. It teaches you how to engage children about what really matters, how to address your child's heart by your words and actions, and how communication and discipline work together when parents love wisely. This book humbled and reminded me that my child will be her own person regardless of what I do. The second is entitled *Strong Fathers, Strong Daughters* by Meg

Meeker, M.D. It taught me that my daughter's world is fragile and tender and we will knead her character as bread dough on a cutting board. Every day she awakens, our hands will pick her up and plop her back down on the board to begin another massage. How I knead her—every single day—will change and shape who she is but still, she will be her own person designed by God Himself.

Sometimes I need to experience the lesson more than once before I fully understand what I'm being taught. The lesson Journey is teaching me at this moment is that she has her own God-given agenda, and I'm just along for the ride. Of course my wife and I are an integral part in shaping and molding this precious child, but at the end of the day, we will need boat loads of patience and understanding when it comes to her development and milestones. On this Joy in the Journey I wouldn't be surprised if I find myself playing the waiting game once again.

Lesson 3

24/7

She's here!!!! She's here!!!

Put me in coach, I'm ready! I remember when I played high school and college football sometimes things would happen that would call for me to be sent to the sideline. Maybe I was winded or the play simply didn't call for me to be on the field at the time. Either way, my play was limited because my abilities weren't always needed. Now I have a new role in life: a role that I have been practicing for my entire life. I will never be called off the field because my new position will always be, Dad.

The entire experience of my wife giving birth to our gorgeous daughter, Journey was absolutely amazing. The feeling I have is like Christmas Day on steroids. I realize that at this moment and for many years to come, I will be like Journey's personal coach helping to develop and shepherd her in life. There will come a time when I will become a general manager, looking from a distance while strategically guiding and supporting her needs versus her wants. Eventually, I will one day simply be a fan cheering and encouraging her from the sideline while she lives her own life. But no matter what cap I may be wearing, nothing will replace my role as always being Journey's Dad.

So how does being an exceptional 24/7-dad look? It looks like living my life with integrity, authenticity, and most importantly, love. These values are integral to my ability to effectively guide and parent Journey. This means that before I can coach or teach anything to better assist in Journey's life, I need to live these values if I want to be able to model them. If I want Journey to show forgiveness to others, then I need to live in a forgiving way. If I want Journey to learn how to set boundaries with others, I need to show how boundaries need to be set. If I want Journey to be a friendly person, then I must live in a friendly and gracious manner. If I want Journey to be fearless when it comes to chasing her dreams, then I need to live by pursuing my dreams with no fear or abandon. And if I want Journey to be able to pick herself up and keep moving forward when she has made a mistake in life, then I need to be willing to pick myself up and keep marching on when times are hard. The one thing I have learned in life is that more is caught than taught. I can't rely on the old cliché "Do what I mean, not what I say". Journey will learn more from my actions than from my words.

Put me in coach, I'm ready 24/7!

Lesson 4

Contentment

Whenever I have heard the word contentment, I've always associated it with weakness, a lack ambition, settling, or being happy with "good enough." Earlier this week, I had the grill fired up and Lionel Richie's "Stuck on you" playing in the background. I looked across the living room at my lovely wife rocking our daughter in her arms, silently praying she falls asleep. I then looked at my mother-in-law, who has been in town giving us extra support and help, as her face beamed with joy. I began to reflect back over the people in my life. I realized at that moment everyone was in good health and my relationships were all in good standing. Then I narrowed my focus on my immediate extended family, my parents, brothers, grandmother, and dearest friends. I began to feel this surge of energy running through my body; it was almost as if I was floating in the air. As I made eye contact back with my wife, Lionel Richie was no longer playing in the background, but I could still hear the song "Stuck on you" loud and clear in my ears. In that very moment, I had it all. I didn't need more or want more. I felt a peace that ran deep down to the core of my bones. I was content.

How could this be? It wasn't like my wife and I had been getting a ton of sleep. I wasn't even in my dream house. I wasn't lying on the beach in the Caribbean drinking a dark and stormy while watching the sunset. I wasn't walking on the 18th fairway at St. Andrews with my childhood buddies. I wasn't in Paris, France or Rome, Italy. I wasn't even debt-free. I didn't have a six-pack of shredded muscles...

There were several times during the recent days since Journey's birth that I had to wipe tears from my wife's eyes because we both knew things were no longer the same. There were moments I've felt guilty because I knew more was being asked of my wife than of me. She is breastfeeding every three hours 24 hours a day and dealing with Journey's colic at night, and all I could offer was a foot massage, diaper changes, and my prayers to God to strengthen my wife and comfort her in this transition of our life. I have gotten the "you've got to be kidding me look" when I said I think I need to get a CrossFit workout in because it had been almost two weeks since I had been to the gym. When she hit me with "Yeah you should go. There's no reason we both should have to suffer," I quickly realized moral support is not to be discounted. "Nevermind, sweetheart. The CrossFit gym can wait."

My days staying up a little later to possibly play a game of John Madden football on my PS3 are over. My previously free time is now filled with reading at least three nursery books to Journey—studies have shown when infant daughters have their fathers read to them, it enhances their development. Right now, sleep is like the golden ticket in Willy Wonka and The Chocolate Factory. When it's available, you take it.

So why am I so content if everything isn't what it seems? Because I'm right with God, myself, my wife, and Journey. When I have those boxes checked off, I have plenty of reasons to feel at peace and that is what contentment means to me.

Lesson 5

Two-Week Check-Up

Am I doing this right?

So many questions concerning Journey have been swirling around our house the last of couple weeks. Is she getting the proper amount of food from breastfeeding? Why does she seem to cry more and have a harder time sleeping during the night than any other time during the day? Has she gained the weight back she lost after the first few days of birth? Has she been peeing and pooping enough? Is it normal for her skin to peel or a tiny rash to appear here or there? How is her overall health?

One day, in the waiting room of the pediatrician's office, I noticed something interesting. They handed my wife a worksheet on a clipboard entitled Edinburgh Postnatal Depression Scale. That's when I realized that the two-week check up wasn't only for Journey. They wanted to know if Mommy was healthy, too. Yes, I have heard of postpartum depression so I made up my own list of things to look for. I call them the "Five S's": sleepy, sad, scared, sappy, and snappy. Daily, I check in with my wife and observe her mood and behavior. I wasn't necessarily shocked about the survey my wife was asked to fill out, but I was taken off guard that it was so up front. It read as follows "As you are pregnant or have recently had a baby, we would like to know how you are feeling. Please check the answers that come closest to how you have felt IN THE PAST 7 DAYS, not just how you feel today."

Here's an example of the ten questions:

> I have felt happy -
> Yes, all the time
> Yes, most of the time

No, not very often
No, not at all

After meeting with the nurse practitioner and having her answer all our questions, my wife and I were told that Journey is a precious, healthy baby developing quite nicely. She had gained a whopping 8 pounds since her birth. As far as her crying, if she had been fed, her diaper had been changed, and she was comforted, her crying was just a baby being a baby. It's all normal, she is just trying to get used to being on dry land. The nurse looked over the questionnaire that my wife had filled out and commented that she was right where she was supposed to be. No red flags. The feelings, concerns, and emotions that had been swirling around our home were all a part of the postpartum process. On the ride home my wife said something very encouraging, "At the end of the day it's all about reassurance and as young parents we just wanted to feel reassured."

I must admit, after reading the survey of questions and thinking of the Five S's, I began having more frequent conversations with my wife about our moods and feelings. I acknowledged that I noticed that I had been feeling a little off lately and to my surprise she did not think that was unusual. I was under the impression that since I was a man that I couldn't be impacted negatively emotionally or mentally by the birth of my child. After all, I was not the one that gave birth to her and had hormonal fluctuations. She informed me that overall it is an adjustment for both parents and it's reasonable to have feelings come up.

I am a ridiculously optimistic person and I know that there is a season for everything under the sun. But to be 100% honest, this is a major adjustment unlike anything I have ever experienced and it changes daily. It is truly no longer about me. I know that Journey is going to mirror and bless my wife and I with many opportunities to view life in a different way. I know it was only a two-week check up, but the saying "one day at a time" has a meaning that now hits closer to home and resonates with me in a whole new way.

Lesson 6

A Community of Love

People say it takes a village to raise a child, and I must say, I have experienced that firsthand in our small Temple community. Over the course of my life, I have had a difficult time accepting compliments and receiving love. I don't know if it's because I'm a middle child or because my parents divorced when I was 4 years old. Either way, I have always felt like I needed to *earn* love. Something had to be done on my part to receive love so I have often found myself trying to please other people. Wanting to prove to them that I was good enough. This was not only the case with people but also with God.

Over the past 2 years, I have reached a place where I've learned that to love is to let go. I've also learned that I cannot control the people who love me—their love is a gift. And as for God's love, I can't ever please, earn, or be good enough for His love. It is a gift and it has nothing to do with me. It's all because He is God.

Imagine the mirror that Journey has held for me to see this reflection of Godly love. We are so blessed to have a community of love and support in this town. My mother in-law has taken 8 weeks off of work to help support the beginning of this new stage in life. We have had multiple other family and friends drive to Temple just to hold Journey for a few minutes. From phone calls and text messages from around the state and country, to neighbors simply wanting to know how we are doing, to the meal train by our Bible study has had for us the last couple of weeks, we have been showered with love and blessings from our community. And this is not because Journey, my wife nor I did something to earn the love of our community; it's just because they are who they are. It's humbling to experience that love firsthand and it's a gentle reminder of the love God shows and demonstrates towards me daily.

Lesson 7

Domesticated

"People who are born round don't die square"-Teddy Atlas

I'm a cliché "family man", and I love it. This week, we made the big move to Tulsa, Oklahoma. I couldn't help but feel like part of a State Farm commercial. You know the one in which the guy is saying things that he's never going to do: he's never going to get married, he's never going to have kids, he's never going to live in the suburbs, never going to get a minivan, he's never going to have a second kid, and then he looks around while holding his children, and he says I'm never going to let go. I'm going to stick by my guns for sure on the never getting a minivan part. I also hope and pray that when we have a second child that will be our max. I'd like to keep man-on-man defense and with more than 2 kids, you have to start playing zone defense. I'm not sure my wife and I could handle playing zone.

Moving and getting acclimated has been an adventure. It's been a hectic week of unpacking boxes in our new home, getting Journey settled, making sure the backyard for our two dogs is secure, and making sure our cat is adjusting emotionally (yes, she's emotional). I definitely don't feel de-masculinized. I don't feel like I'm missing out on life by being a family man. This is my life. It can be challenging, stressful, and difficult at times but it's mine. However, it's evolving, it's rewarding, and it's a blessing. I am now domesticated.

It's all an act of selflessness and service. Serving is the opposite of my natural inclination. Most of the time, I'm more interested in "serve us" than service. I got my first job as a waiter for Pappadeaux Cajun Seafood restaurant when I was 18. Then after I graduated from college, I was a manager for a couple of years at Pappadeaux, receiving numerous service awards along the way. I was also a waiter for the number one steakhouse in the state of Texas under the same Pappas Restaurant umbrella. So I have the experience of knowing what it means to be of service.

When I find myself wanting my way over what's best for my family, this is when I need to stop and take a step back. When the getting gets good, I'm learning to become more aware of moments when I self-sabotage my dreams, life, and family. It's been defined as "When part of your personality acts in conflict with another part of your personality." I do this by dodging emotions, procrastinating, being extremely modest, fearing success, dwelling on too many options, quitting when things gets tough, and telling myself a negative story. I'm reminded of two quotes that help dig me out of this state of being: "God always gives us strength enough and sense enough for everything He want us to do" by John Ruskin and "Our truest life is when we are in dreams awake" by Henry David Thoreau

So at the end of the day, I am embracing my new life and my new state of being as a domesticated man. I will continue on this new adventure and continue to see the joy in the journey.

Lesson 8

Date Night (Safe Night)

"If you live each day as if it was your last someday you most certainly would be right."

I once heard someone say if today were the last day of my life, would I want to do what I'm about to do today? There was a time in life when I felt and thought that I was invincible. I thought nothing could happen that would cause me to die. I thought I was unique and special and could live through anything. Even as I entered into marriage, I felt like I was unbreakable. This way of thinking had allowed me to become arrogant and in some stages of my life irresponsible by doing actions like: not handing my keys over to allow someone else to drive when I know I've probably had one too many to drink, having unprotected sex, not always driving with my seatbelt on, and more recently, being tempted to text while driving. This way of thinking sometimes has a place when I need to motivate and encourage myself to go the distance, for example, if I'm doing a workout, trying something new, or when dealing with business. If this tenacity is not used properly, however, it can be dangerous.

One of the first thoughts that slapped me in the face when I became a father was the thought of my mortality. For one of the first times in my life, I had actually come to the realization that one day, I'm going to die. I knew it was always on the table, obviously, but that still didn't stop me from doing risky and irresponsible things as if I was invincible. I've been married for six years and for six years I've been saying I need to make a will. Have I done it yet? No. Why? Because I think I have enough time to get to it eventually. After having Journey, I've become more aware that I don't have time to waste thinking about "getting to it eventually." I need to get to it now.

This week, Saran and I had our first date night and my mother-in-law graciously volunteered to watch her granddaughter. For the first time in my life, when I walked out of my front door to enjoy a night out on the town with my beautiful wife, the thoughts on my mind weren't about sex after our date, the restaurant, or the food. "I" wasn't even in the equation. The prayer running through my mind first and foremost was God please let us return home safely. I thought how can I put myself in the best possible position to not die or go to jail from thinking I was invincible. My prayer and number one concern was not *I*, but *Journey* and not making her an orphan. Date night was awesome and we both had a blast enjoying each other's company. I am definitely aware that I am mortal and one day I will leave this world. Instead of dwelling on that thought, however, I simply think about our bundle of joy, my beautiful family, and focusing on the joy in the journey.

Lesson 9

Family of Origin

Why do I do the things that I do? It's likely because the apple doesn't fall too far from the tree. I had a conversation with my therapist once and it was centered on the concept of *family of origin*. Family of origin is another term for family tree that encompasses reflecting on your relationships with certain relatives that have impacted your life in various ways. It is about looking in the mirror and seeing who was integral to shaping your life and the person you have become. As you can imagine, that can turn into a heavy conversation and reflection depending on your experiences.

But, back to my therapist. As our conversation on said topic was coming to a close, I made the statement, "Family of origin is no joke", and my therapist chuckled. Needless to say, family of origin is no laughing matter sometimes. There are certain parts of my family and characteristics of my parents that are enduring and that I embrace. My father is very well traveled and charismatic and as I've gotten older, I myself have become well traveled and often been told that I am very charismatic. Also, my mother is especially considerate of other people's feelings and calls often just to see how I am doing. In that same fashion, I have become more aware of other people's feelings, and being a middle child, I'm usually calling to check up on my friends and family frequently.

Earlier this week, I saw *family of origin* in action while at the grocery store with my mother-in-law. She picked up an item in aisle four then realized she no longer wanted the item while she was in aisle five, so she just placed it on the shelf. I picked up the item and said, "Don't worry, your daughter does exact same thing" and I returned the item to aisle four. She looked at me and laughed.

Family of origin is apparent in career drive among relatives as well. My wife's grandmother flew up this week from St. Thomas, USVI to meet her great granddaughter, Journey. As I took a picture of the four generations of women, it was beautiful to see the legacy that has taken shape over time. My wife's grandmother lived a life of service and is now a retired kitchen supervisor. My mother-in-law has served as a registered nurse for the last 36 years. And now my wife has the pleasure to serve as a general cardiologist. Given this trend I know the future is bright and wide open for our 7-week-old daughter, Journey.

But there is a dark and grimy side to the family of origin at times. We have to be extra aware of the mirror our family of origin holds in front of us that reflects the cycle of sin that has been passed on generation after generation. It can be difficult to break this cycle of divorce, secrets, deception, isolation, and even addiction, especially during the holiday season when family is front and center. There can be a back and forth cycle of trying to trust God but then wanting to do it on your own; loving unconditionally, but then setting the conditions; saying you will forgive, but not letting go. This cycle is bigger than you or I. We must go forward with an attitude of unfinished business and perseverance in order to break those cycles that perpetuate in our families. Thanks be to God that He removes us from our sins as far as the east is from the west and He forgets them as deep as the depths of the sea never to be remembered again.

I hold this concept near and dear to my heart because I know that understanding and coping with our family of origin is doing the best that we can with the tools we have, and acceptance is key. I can only imagine what Journey will think the first time she hears someone say "the apple doesn't fall far from the tree." She will inherit both wonderful and not so wonderful traits from her mother and father, but that all goes into the amazingly humbling task of parenting and I look forward to seeing the finished product.

Lesson 10

Isolation vs. Self Centered

Maybe I'm just being too sensitive. It wouldn't be the first time—I mean, I'm a Virgo for goodness sake. It's been said the Virgo man has a cool exterior with a sensitive interior. I just need to suck it up. This is the happiest time of my life. But why do I feel so emotionally heavy? The real question is why do I feel so alone? Maybe I'm just going through a rough week of being a stay-at-home dad.

However, as I begin to Google being a stay-at-home dad, the word that immediately follows is isolation. Here I was thinking I was being too sensitive and was beginning to feel self-centered, but the first article I clicked on was entitled "Breaking through stay-at-home dad isolation." The first two sentences said it all, "One real side effect of being a stay-at-home dad is a feeling of isolation. It can happen to those with the best of intentions and the strongest of wills." People who know me best know that I am an extrovert. A true "people person" in every sense of the word—so much so, that I have often been asked if I had ever met a stranger or a person I didn't like. To answer that question real quick, yes and yes. I do, however, feed off of relationships when I have a genuine connection with the person or a meaningful conversation. It feels as if my soul is nourished when I make those connections. Meaningful for me doesn't necessarily mean that it has to be extra deep. It can be simply discussing your favorite NFL football team or travel, or it can be heavy hitters, like the topics of religion and politics.

The life of a baby is pretty simple and straightforward. If everything is healthy and on the up and up, then it's very routine. Journey pretty much eats and sleeps every three hours. She wakes up, eats again, burps then that's followed by a good poop and pee. She does this about 5 to

6 times a day. My wife has been doing an excellent job producing breast milk, which is no easy task. In between the eating, sleeping, and pooping, there is the washing of bottles. By God's grace and blessings we haven't experienced any significant illnesses at this stage.

They say solitary confinement is the worst punishment a person can receive in prison. After so many days of being alone, the prison begins to drive you insane. I would expect that for a stay-at-home mom, it may be quite different. Just the common bond of being a mother opens up a web of communication and connection with other mothers. My phone doesn't ring often, but when it does, the first question is, "How are Mom and Journey doing?" Again, maybe I'm just being self-centered.

Maybe I wouldn't feel so disconnected and on an island if we were still back in Texas, but moving to a new city after Journey's birth has definitely added to the funk I'm in this week. In Texas, I had a number of opportunities to feel connected via church, Bible studies, CrossFit, golf, and even the people at the local grocery store. I'm thankful that Saran and I have a solid marriage and excellent communication. I'm able to speak openly with her about all of these feelings, and I know that there is a season for everything. This season isn't going to last, and it won't be long until Journey is crawling, walking, and talking. I need to cherish these times.

The stay-at-home dad article on isolation gave some great tools to break through the fog, such as keeping active in your interests, forming or joining a playgroup, finding a stay-at-home social, and talking it out. I've begun to take action by visiting a couple of churches to find a church home, visiting CrossFit gyms, looking for volunteer opportunities in my new community, and reaching out to the local SAHD (stay-at-home dad) and WAHD (work-at-home dad) groups. On a bright note, I met a neighbor a couple doors down this afternoon and he invited me to his church. Any spark is better than no spark in the joy in the journey.

Lesson 11

You Mad Bro?

One recent summer I had my niece and twin nephews visiting for a couple of weeks. At the time, my niece was twelve and my twin nephews were nine. One morning, I woke up and I saw one of my nephews had on a shirt that said, "You mad bro?" My first thought was this is a very sarcastic shirt, but then I quickly realized I was being a stuffy old uncle and I started to laugh. #DontSweattheSmallStuff.

One of the many gifts of having a 2-month-old infant is having an understanding that you must let go of expectations. Over the last couple of years, I have come to realize that most of the time when I become upset or mad it's because of unmet expectations. This is particularly true when it comes to dealing with people; 9 out of 10 times I expect them to do something and it didn't work out the way that I wanted it to and anger follows. This isn't necessarily fair to the other person because most of the time they are living their life unaware of my expectations. If I have an expectation of wanting to get a certain amount of work or things accomplished in a day or week and I'm not able to reach that mark, I have a tendency to become annoyed and easily frustrated, not to mention downright mad at times. This isn't healthy for me (or anyone else for that matter) because I'm wasting energy on being upset, which causes me to shut down. Journey has taught me that less is more and that I need to leave room for flexibility. After all, it isn't about my will, but God's will.

Nothing can get my stress and anxiety from 0 to 100 as quickly as when Journey starts crying. Not because I don't know what to do. I know she's either: hungry, has a dirty diaper, hot, cold, or fighting sleep. However, I haven't spent any serious time around crying babies, so overall it's still new to me. For me to mentally stay engaged and not take her crying personally causes me to feel like the world is caving in on me. To cope, I begin to speak in third person while speaking aloud to my daughter. Something along the lines of "Daddy sees you have a poopy diaper. Let Daddy change your diaper for you." This puts me in the role of Dad and doesn't make it feel like another chore for me to do. It can't be fun and games all the time, but I want to have as much fun as I can. Plus, I've read that holding, talking, cuddling, reading, singing, and playing often with your baby helps build trust between you and your baby.

I couldn't help thinking back to my nephew's shirt (*You mad bro*) while I was recently feeding Journey at 3:00am (on a side note, I haven't seen 3 AM this many times sober in my life). In a matter of 15 minutes, I had been vomited on, sneezed on directly in my face, and somehow pooped on from her poop managing to ooze out of her diaper and down my stomach. In another life, I definitely would have been mad. Being that it was my daughter, just made me laugh out loud. I told her she could vomit, sneeze, and poop on Daddy whenever she'd like to. Journey is now at the cooing stage, so she loves our little baby talk conversations.

On Monday, Journey had her check up where she got her 2-month shots. Just like her daddy, she isn't a fan of needles. After seeing the tears roll down Journey's chubby little cheeks as she yelled unmercifully to a level her mother and I had never heard before, I thought to myself, *you mad girl?* It brought joy to my heart that we as her parents were there to comfort her.

Lesson 12

All Eyez On Me

In the mid-1990s at the height of his success, the rapper Tupac Shakur released an album entitled "All eyez on Me." All Eyez On Me is 2Pac's best selling album. The album is frequently recognized as one of the crowning achievements of 1990s rap music.

Earlier this week, I was cooking lunch in the kitchen and I noticed Journey was intently focused on me while lying in her bassinet. She was a little fussy, so I figured if I placed her near the kitchen, she could see what was going on maybe she would clam down—she did. As I was seasoning ground turkey, I looked over my shoulder and I noticed that her eyez were following every move that I made. I thought to myself "All eyez on me." For a brief moment, I felt a feeling of pressure thinking how much I did not want to disappoint Journey. Then I felt a feeling of warmth and comfort and a keen sense of awareness that I had never experienced.

All Journey wanted was to be in the presence of her "father." She had her eyez fixed on me. In the very same sense, this is what God wants from you and I. He wants us to be in His presence. The only time Journey would become agitated was when she wasn't able to see me in her space. I thought to myself, how many in my life has Jesus wanted "All Eyez On Him" when But instead of trusting and looking to Him when life begins to squeeze me and become difficult, I become more afraid, I became more doubtful, I begin to worry more, and I want to numb out all together? While standing in my kitchen, I asked myself how can I spend more time with God to strengthen His presence? The answer is that it comes by me reading my Bible, continuing to look for a new church here in Owasso, praying, speaking with both believers and non-believers, and by simply seeking, knocking, and asking. Truth be told, Journey doesn't require me to do anything special in order to strengthen our connection. She just wants us to spend time together.

That same day, while having dinner with my wife, Saran, she commented that she couldn't look at Journey for very long or else she would start crying because she cares for our daughter so much. I gently affirmed my wife and told her to go ahead and cry if that's what was in her heart to do. I continued to ponder my wife's words and eventually had an amazing thought. I thanked Saran for the gift she gave me that day. I told her the reason she wants to cry for Journey when she fixes her eyez on her is because of the deep love she has for her daughter. This is the same way that God cries for all of His children. I feel that it breaks His heart and He cries even deeper when we sin and don't repent, when we hurt one another (not just as husband and wife, but the entire world), and when we turn from Him altogether. I was so thankful for this illustration.

That entire day was a very humbling experience. Journey and Saran both keep the joy in my life coming in ways I've never dreamed possible. So often, I get lost in the busyness of life, but on this particular day, I was reminded of something very important...All Eyez On Him.

Lesson 13

Pacifier

Whenever I think of a baby with its pacifier, the character Linus from Charlie Brown is often the first thing that pops into my head. Lee Mendelson, producer of the majority of the *Peanuts* television specials, has said that Linus is his favorite character:"He made sucking your thumb and holding a security blank OK." To my 11-week-old daughter, Journey, her pacifier brings her both comfort and security all at the same time. The decision to use a pacifier—or not—is up to you. For my wife and I it's a must have, ranking right up there with diaper wipes and her bassinet.

I did a little research on pacifiers and found that for some babies, pacifiers are the key to contentment between feedings. Babies are happiest when they are sucking something. Consider the advantages: pacifiers can be a temporary way to distract and sooth a fussy baby, help your baby fall asleep, ease discomfort during flying, and even help reduce the risk of sudden infant death syndrome. Of course, pacifiers have pitfalls as well. Some drawbacks include possible interference with breast-feeding, dependence on the pacifier, increased risk of middle ear infections, and possible increased risk of dental problems.

Pacifier do's and don'ts:

- Wait until breast-feeding is well-established

- Don't use a pacifier as a first line of defense

- Choose the silicone one-piece, dishwasher-safe variety

- Let your baby set the pace

- Keep it clean

- Don't sugarcoat it

- Keep it safe

So, when do you pull the plug on the pacifier? The risks of pacifier use begin to outweigh the benefits as babies get older. While most kids stop using pacifiers on their own between ages 2 and 4, others need help breaking the habit.

I couldn't help but ask myself the question: Do I still use a pacifier? Where do I run to or have run to for comfort as an adult? Melatonin supplements, alcohol, women, or other inappropriate things. I have weaned myself from things that brought me comfort as a child, but as an adult, now they no longer give those benefits. I have learned that my ultimate comfort comes from God. As amazing as my spouse is and as much as I love my career, they can't be there to comfort me all of the time. Because I know where my true comfort comes from, I know Journey will also experience His comfort. That thought fills my heart with joy.

Lesson 14

Studying

"We enjoy discovering as much as we can about things we truly care about. If it's our favorite football team, we'll read any article that helps us keep up with how they're doing. If it's cooking, we'll check out those channels or Web sites that share the best grilling techniques or dessert recipes. If there's a subject that appeals to us, we'll take notice any time it comes up. In fact, it naturally becomes our area of personal study."-The Love Dare

Studying has never been high on my list of things to do. Maybe it's due to the fact that I didn't discover that I was dyslexic until I was a junior at Hardin-Simmons University or that I didn't learn I had ADHD until I was 30. I do, however, have a passion for learning and the curiosity to try new things. If I really had to narrow it down and put my finger on it, studying and learning, especially when it comes to people, brings me excitement. This is why I majored in psychology and have a Bachelor's degree in behavioral science.

I had an interesting conversation with my mother-in law this week. She had flown up from Texas to spend a few days with her one and only grandchild (can't beat a grandmother's love). She commented that Journey and I were going to have such a great bond because we get to spend so much time together. Being a stay-at-home dad has many unique advantages and one of them is getting to truly study and learn my daughter's behavior and personality.

A couple of years ago, I was reading the book *The Love Dare* and taking the challenges along the way to help build a closer marriage between Saran and myself. One of the dares was "Love seeks to understand." In this dare the authors said, "Consider the following perspective: if the amount you studied your spouse before marriage were equal to a high school diploma, then you should continue to learn about your mate until you gain a college degree, a master's degree, and ultimately a doctorate degree. Think of it as a lifelong journey that draws your heart closer to your mate."

I was once a child and I have spent enough time studying kids. I have especially paid close attention to my niece and twin nephews and have learned that love isn't spelled "M-O-N-E-Y", but more like "T-I-M-E." To go further, spending quality time with Journey is not the end goal; it is only the vehicle to achieve my goal. To have quality trust from my daughter is the true goal, which is cultivated by spending that time with her. While she is only 12 weeks old, at this stage of her development, I'm more or less studying and observing her mannerisms to have a solid understanding of what she is trying to communicate through her body language, crying, and cooing. I'm becoming better at learning her behavior. During the next stage in her development I will go beyond just observing and delve more into inquiring. Asking questions like, "What are your biggest fears?", "What do you love to do the most?", and "What are your dreams and goals?" As the stages progress and time moves on, our relationship will involve me talking less and listening a lot more. The test lies in studying and learning Journey to the point where I can spot when her behavior is incongruent with her personality and she isn't being consistent in her actions. Being her father, I want to be able to notice when things seem off.

However, there is a common pitfall to avoid: I need to be more mindful of distractions that can deter me from accomplishing my goals for our relationship. As my big mama used to tell me, "Too much of a good thing can become bad for you", i.e. social media, my iPhone, my PS4, writing, or even CrossFit. Timothy Keller wrote a great book entitled *Counterfeit Gods* that discusses how anything on earth can become an idol. So as I study and learn Journey, I have to first continue to study and learn about God and my spouse. The action of placing God over everything allows me to have balance in ways I've never dreamed possible. I will continue to take in all the time I can with my daughter day by day and earn my doctorate degree during my joy in the journey.

Lesson 15

Family

"So they are no longer two, but one. Therefore what God has joined together, let no separate." Matthew 19:6

In my experience in life, I've come to believe that a wedding is just for a moment, but a marriage is for a lifetime. With that being said, if Journey is anything like her father (who has been to known to be very extravagant at times), I'm going to have my hands full when it comes to paying for her wedding. Furthermore, if proper attention isn't paid to the marriage, then one of the key components can be overlooked which is "leaving and cleaving." This is something that is not easily done, but is a must if a strong bond is to be established with your spouse. Saran is an only child and I am a middle child out of three boys. With those types of statistics we were doomed for failure. However by God's grace, I think we both have done an exceptional job when he comes to leaving and cleaving while building our unity in our marriage.

At several points during this holiday season, I have made the effort to see how this experience may look through Journey's eyes. Obviously, I'm not expecting her to remember her first experience of the holidays, but I hope that she can feel the level of closeness her mother and I have in our marriage. I myself, have begun to experience a deeper level in leaving and cleaving in establishing our core family.

Anyone who truly knows me, knows that I love hosting. I truly find pleasure in serving so I enjoy a house full of people. I relish the opportunity to cook a delicious meal and build memories. But one of the drawbacks in all the excitement is that I can unconsciously lose sight of the core meaning of the entire experience. Being a middle child, I can get caught up in wanting to make everybody happy causing me to disconnect and make me lose the *why* in my actions. Saran and Journey are reminders to me—especially during the holiday season—that at the end of the day, regardless of what is going on around us, it comes down to the three of us. Simply put, "leaving and cleaving" means that my core family is now comprised of Saran, Journey, and myself. This may seem a little strong, but for me, it's a concept that I need to hear and stay connected to.

During the last 6 1/2 years of being married, I understand the unity of our marriage more and more each day. There are many different obstacles and challenges in life that can draw you closer to your spouse: the loss of a job, the loss of a parent, addiction, etc. Any level of brokenness where a couple reaches a point when they no longer just choose to be married, but instead thrive in marriage while seeing God take their worst and turn it into His best is a vehicle to ultimate unity in marriage. I believe experiencing the birth of Journey has deepened our oneness in leaving and cleaving in ways that I never dreamed possible. The personal note that my mom left on the bottom of my Christmas card really helped to solidify and illustrate my version of leaving and cleaving: "Merry Christmas son and thanks for an awesome visit with you and your family."

Lesson 16

Less is more

I have been praying on a motto to adopt for the New Year and I believe that motto will be "Less is more." At this particular stage in life, I don't see it being very smart or wise to plan a lot of things to get done throughout the day and end up not being able to accomplish them. When I plan a whole day and I don't get to everything, it causes me to become very frustrated and feel like I am slacking. My new goal is to pick one or two major things. They may be as simple as just trying to get a workout in or getting the laundry done. Once those one or two things are accomplished I can then allow myself to relax. The main point of the game is to be flexible and present for Journey.

I try not to make New Year's resolutions, but rather make goals that I want to accomplish throughout the year. Some may be small, some medium, and some lofty. I review my goals weekly and I purposely make small goals that lead into large ones to psychologically build momentum. Last year I accomplished almost 90% of my goals. At the end of a year, I want to be able to look back and see and know that I got better. I'm also the guy with a bucket list. I'm the guy that at the beginning of the year 2000 I made a list of things that I want accomplished in the next 10 years. So it goes without saying that I love my lists and I am a goal-oriented person. It has a lot of positive qualities, like giving me the ability to be self-motivated and very driven.

But being so goal-oriented also comes with some shortcomings. Sometimes I can get too focused and become narrow-minded. Sometimes I can become so driven that I don't leave margins for error. I can be so consumed with getting my list accomplished that I lose sight of the enjoyment in the little things. The biggest shortcoming that I am finally getting better at learning is making sure my day has God first. The wrong way would involve me making my list and acting as if God was Genie from the movie Aladdin—I would expect Him to just make it happen. If it didn't happen, I would take it personally and feel as if something was wrong with me. I would also compare myself to other people. Obviously none of those ideas are going to come out with good results. I've often heard it said, "If you want to make God laugh tell Him your plans."

The reason less is more is so important as my theme for this year because I don't want to lose sight of what's truly important and I do not want to overlook God's presence in my everyday life. When it comes to Journey, she will likely be identified as a Daddy's girl. However, as both of us grow older in life, I would love to feel that "Daddy's girl" is just a bond of trust and security where Journey feels supported and loved. A space where she feels that she can be herself, be honest, and we can share life's moments as she becomes a young woman. If I'm caught up and too involved in trying to accomplish my list for the day, I will be pulled in too many directions and I'm not going to be able to make myself available fully to what's important. Less is more gives me room for flexibility. I'm not a fan of anything that can lead to distracting me from what's important in my life. I simply ask God to let His will be done and I continue my joy in the journey.

Lesson 17

Babysitter

This week, Saran and are preparing to venture out onto a new frontier: finding a babysitter. Until now, we really haven't thought much about someone nor have we needed anyone. My mother-in-law has been flying up from Texas once or twice a month and stays about three to four days. This has allowed Saran and I to go out to dinner and have a nice date night from time to time. During the day, I could catch a CrossFit workout, go watch a matinee movie, or if I really wanted to, live out on the edge, go grocery shopping all by myself.

However, this week we have some friends coming into town for a job interview with the same company that Saran works for. It's been arranged for us to all go out to dinner together on—wait for it—a Friday night! My mother-in-law is not going to be in town, hence, our search for a sitter has started. Now that Journey is almost four months old and has a few shots under her belt, it seems that it's time to look for a babysitter. Here we are in a new city, with no family, and trying to build a family. What, where, and how are a few of the immediate questions that pop into my head when it comes to even thinking about going down the path of looking for a babysitter. What's the best way to go about starting to look for a babysitter? Well, Google of course.

Care.com ranks at the top of the search and to make it easier they have a put together a list of 19 things to look for in a babysitter: flexibility, patience, attentiveness, enjoys children, bilingual, trustworthy, safety conscious, loving, enthusiastic, athletic, honest, good communicator, experienced, creative, funny, tidy, practical, healthy, and reliable. Okay, I think that's a pretty good starting point.

Urbansitter blog also put together a pretty solid list: Do you feel comfortable and safe leaving your kids with them? Do they get good reviews from your kids? Do they speak another language fluently? Do they speak English as their first language? Will they do laundry? Will they run errands? Will they take the kids outside? Do they love arts and crafts projects? Will they spoil your kids? Are they able to follow your discipline style? Do they like helping kids with homework? Are they a type-A personality just like you? Can they cook or bake? I feel like this list is more for Mrs. Doubtfire than for a babysitter. All we need is a couple of hours for dinner not a caregiver until Journey graduates from high school.

After reading over these lists, I've concluded the best course of action is to pick the top three to five things off our list that our family feels is most important. I find it interesting that neither list mentioned anything about faith. As I've gotten older in life and spend more time reading and strengthening my relationship with God, I don't always do a good job in this particular area. But over the last year, I've learned a powerful lesson that obedience is better than sacrifice. Our reality is that we moved to an entirely different state where we have no friends or family to pursue a career and start building a family, and out of all the states in America, it happens to be Oklahoma. If you are a true Texan like my wife and myself, then I don't have to waste a lot of time explaining how you just don't cross the Red River and move to Oklahoma. But the truth of the matter is, we moved here completely out of obedience in our faith not sacrifice. Speaking from a place of humility, the entire transition as a whole has been practically seamless.

It fills our hearts with joy that the first major relationship that we have started to build happens to be a very close friend of my wife's best friend's mom. Their friendship goes back over 40 years. This connection does not just happen by accident. The fact that she is a strong, Christian woman in her faith doesn't just add to the icing on the cake, but it *makes* the cake. She has two daughters of her own who are more than capable of taking care of Journey. I'd say through faith our search is over. #BabysittersCheck

Lesson 18

No End In Sight

Journey is now four months old, and I have officially realized that the train has definitely left the station. There's no end in sight. I know this may sound very obvious to people that are already parents. I acknowledge the fact that it may seem I should've already known this by now. However, the truth of the matter is that it has taken me four months to learn that there is no day off in being a parent.

Almost everything I've ever been a part of in my life has had a start and a finish. Whether I was a part of athletics in high school or playing collegiate football, there was always a start to the season and an end to the season. When I begin reading a book, there's a beginning and there is an end. Whenever I have started a diet or a fast, there's always been an end point. It may have taken me five years to graduate from college, but eventually I finished. I once ran a marathon and it took me 5 1/2 hours to cross the finish line, but thank God, that too came to an end.

There are only a couple of things that come to my mind when I think of things that have no ending. The first would be marriage. If you want to get technical, death technically ends a marriage, but I pray that I am married to my spouse until the day I die. In that case, whoever is called to glory first, an end will take place. The second is any form of addiction and recovery. By this I mean the 12 steps of recovery will never have an end to them if a person or individual wants to continue to live a life of sobriety and have recovery.

I guess the reason that it feels like there is no end in sight is because every morning starts off with a feeling of Groundhog Day. No matter what is going on at around 4:30 AM Journey begins to wake up and as I sit on the edge of the bed before I get up to go prepare her bottle, I can't help but say to myself, "Am I doing this all over again?"

There are a lot of steps and responsibilities in maintaining the growth and survival of an infant. And quite frankly, it seems very overwhelming at times. By God's grace I've been able to sustain and hold on to the little bit of sanity that I have. I feel like my spouse and I are in the process of starting a garden when it comes to being the parents of Journey. Yes, there will be a time where we will just be sitting back watching her bloom and blossom into whatever it is that God has created her to become. But at our current stage in life, I feel like we're just beginning to dig the soil. We won't be digging forever, but right now, it feels like that's all were doing.

A few weeks ago, we increased our life insurance policy in case something ever happens to us so that Journey will be well taken care of. The nurse that came to our home to do our labs and fill out the paperwork asked me what my profession was so she could document it. I have never been happier and prouder in my life to say "homemaker." Sometimes I feel absolutely awful as a parent and wonder what type of impact I am having on my infant daughter. For example, when I'm wrapped up in the process of making Journey's bottle while trying to do the laundry, and then the doorbell rings while she is in the background screaming bloody murder because she's hungry, I feel awful that Journey has to wait a few extra minutes for her bottle and in the process, she's getting all worked up with her crying. Maybe I'm being a little too hard on myself, however these are the type of feelings that can sometimes make me feel like am I doing this the wrong way.

This weekend, I'm going back to Texas to attend an annual men's retreat. It's a great opportunity for me to be around other God-fearing men to help strengthen one another both mentally and spiritually. I'm a firm believer that iron sharpens iron. I'm also anticipating getting a few extra hours of sleep as well as sleeping in a bed without Journey in between my wife and me. This will be my first time staying away from Saran and

Journey since Journey was born. There's a part of me that can't wait to get back home to be close to my lovely wife and beautiful daughter. This will be the first time in my life that I will be returning from a trip to walk into my home and be greeted by my new family.

So yes, the "lifetime of parenthood" train has officially left the station and it doesn't look like there is an end in sight. But there isn't enough money in the world that would make me want to get off this train on any stop along the way.

Lesson 19

Honey, I'm Home

For the first time since Journey has been born, I stayed the night away from my spouse and my daughter. I recently flew back to Texas for a men's conference and while I was excited about being back in my hometown, seeing close family and friends, and more importantly, sleeping longer than four hours straight, a part of me secretly wondered what I would miss while I was gone.

The 29th annual Central Texas men's conference was taking place in Giddings Texas at Camp Tejas. The theme for the conference was entitled "Life is calling." I knew what was calling me—I felt like a kid on Christmas because I knew that I was getting ready to enjoy unrestricted sleep. For many men attending the conference, they were excited about an unrestricted curfew. The basketball court was lit up, the disc golf course was in swing, and guys were getting ready to play cards and dominoes. Many men were brewing cups of coffee getting ready for a nice long night of catching up with one another. I, however, had other plans in mind...

As I took out my contacts lenses and put on my glasses, I relished in the quietness of the room. As I made my way to bed, I made a phone call to Saran to wish her a good night. I asked her how Journey was doing and whether she seemed to miss me. We made small talk and I thanked her for supporting me in becoming a better man, husband, father, and neighbor. We said I love you and I prayed for our family. With a kiss good night I hung up the phone and got ready to enter Never-never land. Waking up the next morning, I couldn't help but laugh out loud. I thought to myself here I am sharing a cabin with five other men—one dad had four daughters from ages 1 to 9, another dad had five kids, the oldest of which had just become a teenager. The other three dads all had at least two kids each. I'm the one with the four-month-old daughter and I was the first one to go to bed.

I told my roommates for the weekend that I had yet to develop my parenting stamina. One of the dads informed me I probably wouldn't get back all the sleep that I had lost since becoming a dad. As he was laughing at me, he went on to say that he has given up on getting his sleep back and now is just happy to have a few moments of freedom.

Sunday morning, I woke up chomping at the bit ready to get home and share all the new information that I'd learned. I know that I have a tendency to become over eager, to pour everything into life and try to get it all done in a day. Journey is only four months so I still need to pace myself and live life on God's terms. So with all the excitement from the knowledge and experience of the weekend, I have to remind myself to take each day one day at a time. I asked one of the men attending the conference what was the most important thing I should be doing for my daughter right now. He simply said pray for her. Well, I was happy that I had been doing that since the moment I found out we were having a baby. Some other advice I received was to be gentle with myself and understand that it is good that I have a sensitive heart and strive be a good father. They also told me to give myself permission to make mistakes.

As I returned home and peeled into our driveway from the conference, I couldn't help but think how happy Journey would be to see me. As I opened the front door and prepared to say "Honey, I'm home", my beautiful wife greeted me at the door with a smile, a kiss, and a hug. As I walked into the room to say hello to Journey though, I suddenly realized that maybe she might not be happy to see me or she might not remember me, so I quickly prepared myself for her reaction. When her eyes met mine she became startled, her bottom lip began to quiver, and she prepared herself to cry. I knew at that moment that she had known that I was gone, but didn't know when I would return. I know she missed me but I also know that she didn't understand the feelings that she was feeling inside. I hugged her tight and gave her a kiss. She really didn't want to have anything to do with me. She was quite upset with her dad. But over the course of 20 minutes or so, she began to ease up and by the next day, all was right in the world because joy had returned to the journey.

Lesson 20

Never Awake A Sleeping Baby

Parenting means a lot of different things. For me this week it means doing what is hard and difficult while keeping the big picture in mind, which is the overall well-being of Journey. Over the last three months, Journey has spoiled my wife and I rotten when it comes to getting a good night's sleep—well, spoiled us as much as possible when it comes to getting a good night's sleep with a newborn. We had become accustomed to Journey going to bed around <u>10 PM</u> and waking up anywhere <u>between 4:30 AM and 6:00 AM</u>. But that has all changed over the past two weeks. I have gotten slapped right in the face with a firm reminder that the life of a baby is constantly changing. Journey is now waking up from around <u>12:30 AM</u>-<u>1:30 AM</u>, and again around 4 AM to 5:30 AM. That may not sound like a lot and I know others have it much worse, but that extra waking is kicking my butt.

So I finally decided to click "purchase" on that baby sleeping book I save on Amazon. We bought a book entitled "Healthy Sleep Habits, Happy Child." I even felt great to have the reassurance from our pediatrician that this was a good book. One of the first things I learned is that when it comes to sleep and a baby, logic gets tossed out the window because it's all biological. One concept is trying to get Journey to go to bed earlier because in theory, more sleep produces more sleep and hopefully in turn, sleep will be longer without interruptions. If only it was that easy…

Another method is to place your child in their bassinet and walk out of the room and don't return until five minutes has passed. You then return to the room, gently comfort her without making eye contact, and once again leave the room. You now wait until 10 minutes have passed to return to the room if she is still crying, comfort her once again, and continue increasing the timing until the baby falls completely asleep. The first night can take up to 55 minutes, but night after night, the time should decrease until the baby is able to fall asleep on her own.

I can honestly say nothing was more painful than hearing Journey cry at the top of her lungs wanting her mom and me to return to the room. The toughest part was looking at the range of emotions that my spouse was experiencing. She began to cry from the emotions that she was feeling. I read in the book that the mom will often experience a range of emotions from guilt to sadness. We didn't last very long the first night— my wife said enough is enough, and went in to comfort Journey almost immediately. We both didn't realize breaking the cycle that we had started would be this difficult. But returning to the room too early actually made it even longer and harder for her to go to sleep…ouch.

So after reading through this book and feeling like we were the worst parents in the world, we began calling our friends that had recently had children and asking their advice and methods. All of them started the conversation off with a big sigh and a chuckle, followed by the sentiment "good luck." No one had a clear-cut answer or solution! If anything was learned from these conversations it was that we were normal and we weren't alone. This is going to take some time and there is no quick fix. There are many different options and methods and every baby responds to these methods differently. The next book we purchased was entitled "Baby Wise." This book is a little more rigid than the first one and the frustrating thing is that both books seem to contradict one another.

I do feel happy that even though we are on this journey of sleep deprivation that I am blessed enough to be going through it with my wife. It's amazing sometimes to think of how awesome God is. He gave me the exact amount of strength I need to accomplish my goals. I never thought that I could function off two hours of sleep, but miraculously, I'm still able to do what's needed to care for our daughter. We are definitely a long way from sleeping peacefully through the night, but one of the most important things I believe that my spouse and I can do is be a constant and consistent support for one another with whatever sleep plan we decide. It's also important to have the other family members (particularly grandmothers) involved and helping to stick to the plan. Once we get going, there are so many things they can easily set us back, such as Journey getting sick, vacations, friends visiting, etc. Right now, that Motel 6 commercial sounds so sweet to me, but I will continue to sleepily weave my way through this joy in the journey.

Lesson 21

Be My Valentine

What a difference a year can make. Last year during Valentine's weekend, Saran was still early in her pregnancy and we used that weekend to share with our family and friends the good news that God had blessed us with a child. During the same weekend, we visited one of our close couple friends who have now just welcomed their baby girl into this world. Love was definitely in the air.

Fast-forward to a year later and our daughter, Journey is leaving her thumbprints all over our hearts. Not to mention, she has been running me through the paces of being a stay-at-home dad. Unbeknownst to me, my wife had set up for my mother-in-law to fly up and watch after her granddaughter for Valentine's weekend. My spouse walked in from work on Friday evening and to my surprise, simply said, "pack a bag." From there, my mind was racing with a whirlwind of thoughts: Are we flying or driving? When are we coming back? Will I need a jacket? How many pair of underwear do I need?

My wife is a woman who doesn't care a lot about Valentine's Day. A box of chocolates normally suits her just fine. I've been known to go a little over-the-top though, meaning I don't stop with just chocolate. I typically try to stay away from the cliché lingerie gift as well. But I definitely love giving cards, maybe some perfume, and no matter what: romance, romance, and more romance. Needless to say, I was shocked when she was the one taking control of the weekend.

I felt so blessed to have my mother-in-law willing to watch after Journey the entire weekend. I absolutely enjoy being a stay-at-home dad, but it is the most demanding 24/7 commitment I have been blessed with. My spouse used this year's Valentine's weekend to spoil me rotten and shower me with love. Talk about humility. Journey didn't ask to be born, nor for me to be her father. I shouldn't expect a treat for taking care of my daughter, because it goes without saying that it is my duty and privilege. I will be honest with you, though, and tell you that being a parent is harder than I thought it would be, but that doesn't mean that I'm entitled to anything. I'm so thankful to God that he blessed me with a spouse who is so understanding and goes above and beyond to hit my bullseye of love by showing me appreciation, affection, and attention. I'm not the easiest person to be married to and I know I can be a little high maintenance and overbearing. In the same token, I'm grateful that over the course of time, God has widened my awareness on how fortunate I truly am. Also, I can see in the way my daughter looks at me that I am her first love.

So I look forward to continuing to buy flowers and express my love to my wonderful spouse, but to also express that love to my growing daughter every Valentine's Day. On a side note, I'm going to have to make sure I go above and beyond on Mother's Day. But overall, Valentine's Day or Mother's Day or any other holiday is not all about a date on a calendar, but more importantly they are a reminder to show love and appreciation all year long. I want Journey to witness and understand unconditional love through my example of loving her mother day in and day out.

Lesson 22

Home Is Where the Heart Is

Decisions, decisions, decisions…sometimes life just seems like a series of decisions. There are not too many things I dislike more than packing and moving. Last year, in the course of three months my spouse and I moved two times. My wife was eight months pregnant during the first move, and Journey was only a month old during the second one.

When Saran and I were going through our premarital class, the couple that led the class warned us with words of caution saying, "Be careful when stating absolute things you won't do or put up with, particularly when it comes to your marriage." After we finally got unpacked and settled into the home we are currently renting, I breathed a big sigh of exhaustion and relief and told my wife we were not moving anytime soon. Fast-forward to three months later, and we have just met with our realtor/friend who shed light on the possibility of purchasing our first home.

One of the first things that we are learning (and when I say *we*, I mean myself in particular) is that it's easier to move when Journey is an infant than when she is school-aged. Right now for her, home is where the heart is. As long as she feels the love from her mother and I, the home doesn't make a difference. When she is older, it could become more complicated with the loss of friends, the pressure of making new friends, getting use to a new neighborhood, new schools, etc. Moving right now, or in the near future, would impact my wife and me mainly. We like our current location, however most of the people we have met thus far live in a completely different area of town. Also, as Journey gets older, we want her to experience diversity in her life and in this area that is lacking. I grew up around people of various backgrounds during in my childhood, and I feel it's one of the reasons I am so open hearted and have a love for many types of people, culture, and tradition today.

Some things that I've never even considered in my adult life now seem to come to the forefront as a parent. Questions like what is Saran's commute time to work, where is the best school district, the best teachers, the safest neighborhood, distance to church, distance to grocery stores, and on and on. It's a blessing to be in a position in life where God has allowed my bride and me to have the financial means to move if we choose to as well as have the guidance of people who continue to pour knowledge into us to make the best decisions possible. The first question that must be asked is what's best for Journey. Before I became a dad, that would not have been the first question I would have considered when deciding whether to move or not. My spouse and I will be married seven years this May and at risk of sounding sappy, if home is where the heart is, wherever Saran and Journey are is the perfect home for me.

Lesson 23

A Breakthrough

"Sleep training" doesn't have to be hell. It works! She was ready. You were ready."-Sarah Branion

This week was a week of many firsts. After three consecutive nights of getting 3 hours of sleep or less, it was time for my spouse and me to surrender to what was no longer working and transition to sleep training for Journey. Saran began digging deeper into her reading about sleep training and I called on very close friend with a special interest in infant sleep.

During the process, Journey quickly began to set new benchmarks and rise to the occasion. She was at the proper age to start sleep training, which is between three to six months. There are also parameters for a healthy baby weight prior to starting sleep training to ensure your baby has enough nutrients and a sustainable size. Ideally, you want your baby to weigh at least 12 pounds. Journey is a little over 14 pounds, so we checked the box there. During this process you will also be weaning your baby from the middle of the night feeding. Fortunately for us, Journey had gradually done this on her own about a month ago. You are also advised to increase the number of ounces of breast milk or formula your baby is drinking in a day, with the magic number being at least 24 ounces. This is to make sure you are providing the proper amount of calories to aid in the sleep process. Ideally, it's suggested that the night sleep is conquered first because babies treat night and day sleep differently. Maybe it's because I'm dyslexic or because sometimes I just simply do things backwards, but we actually conquered the day sleep slightly before night sleep.

After speaking with my close friend, she helped me understand more about how babies think. For example, babies like to anticipate what's going to happen next. If they can feel like they know what's about to happen, they're more likely to adjust easier. She suggested we implement a day schedule that consisted of a morning bottle followed by a little playtime and then down for a nap. This was then repeated throughout the day. Early evening, we would then slowly transition into the bed routine. We learned a good bedtime routine should have at least five steps.

For us it looked something like this:

1. Bath - Daddy

2. Lotion/pajamas - Mommy

3. Bottle - Mommy

4. Read 2 books - Daddy

5. Prayer - Both

6. Place her down in her bed and walk away

The first three nights of this process, we placed Journey in her co-sleeper basket on our bed to sleep. To our amazement, she slept from 8:40 PM to 7:00 AM. It seems as if Journey was waiting on us all along to allow her to grow and learn on her own. For babies, learning how to sleep is a skill just like learning how to walk and talk.

The results from this new transition have been amazing. Journey is now having regular bowel movements, she is no longer using her pacifier, she has transitioned to sleeping in her actual room, her naps are longer, she is sleeping consistently through the night, and she rolls over to sleep on her stomach when she wants.

A final component that I learned is to be mindful of the word "crying" because if Journey has a fresh diaper, she's had a bottle, and she's comfortable then she is not crying—she is technically fussing. It may seen like a non-important word change, but avoiding the word crying can help to avoid triggers of feeling like something is wrong with Journey. Fussing allows us both to understand that she's OK and she's simply learning a new skill. As parents, it's important to have a mantra and the understanding that this is for her benefit and for the good of her overall health. As Journey continues to grow, my love for her also grows deeper and deeper. After having four nights of great sleep, I love her more and more.

Lesson 24

Daddy & Daughter Weekend

"When you have food for the day at the start of the day and a change of clothes you are a rich man." -Mosaic Law

When you have your basic needs met in life, everything else is extra. My spouse went on a recent girls trip for an extended weekend, so while she was away, it was an opportunity for me to soak up some father-daughter time. One of the things that I want to remember as I continue this journey with my daughter is to see the world through her eyes. I don't want to focus so much on getting her to understand my world, but for me to slow down, be present, and understand *her* world.

How does she interpret things? How does she interpret love, comfort, security, happiness, joy, fear, stress? At five months, she is unable to use the words to express what she is actually feeling, but that doesn't mean she can't *show* what she's feeling. She may be fussy because it's time to take a nap, or she can become stressed if it's been too long between bottle feedings, or she can feel confident being held by her mother, and secure while looking in the eyes of her father.

At this stage, if I stripped down our daily activity together to the bare bones, it's as simple as feeding Journey, changing her diapers, ensuring she has some tummy time, allowing her a few naps, and helping her get a good night's sleep. Everything else is extra. We praise God that we have a healthy baby. I know that we are blessed and that's not always the case with other families. At the end of the day, all we really need is food, shelter, and a change of clothes to have a blessed day.

Journey now realizes where sounds come from, and she'll turn quickly toward a new one. Sometimes if I want to engage her I jingle my keys or squeeze Sophie the giraffe. Journey has gotten to the point were she is now able to recognize her own name and understand that I'm speaking to her when I say it. She turns her head when I call her or talk about her with others. If I want to engage and entertain Journey, all I need to do is talk to her. At this age, babies don't learn language from the television or radio, so it's important to turn off the electronics and use in-person dialogue instead.

Journey has also been showing strong attachment by raising her arms when she wants to be picked up and by crying when her mom or I leave the room. She loves giving hugs and kisses. She is beginning to understand jokes by laughing at the funny expressions. An oldie but a goodie around the Oliver house lately has been the classic peekaboo. Journey really soaks it up with a cute giggle and a gorgeous smile.

I look forward to many more opportunities for us to have father-daughter weekends together. I'm thankful that God has given me a heart to truly want to be a father. I feel like the richest man on earth.

Lesson 25

Ain't No Mountain High Enough

In 1967, Marvin Gaye and Tammi Terrell released a song called "Ain't No Mountain High Enough" from their United album. It was an instant hit. Later, Diana Ross from the Supremes recorded it again. It was her first solo number-one hit on the billboard hot 100 chart and was nominated for a Grammy. Here are the opening lyrics to this classic song:

"Listen baby, ain't no mountain high,

> Ain't no valley low, ain't no river wide enough baby.
>
> If you need me call me, no matter where you are,
>
> No matter how far; don't worry baby
>
> Just call my name; I'll be there in a hurry
>
> You don't have to worry,"

You may be thinking what does a kid that was born in 1979 know about Marvin Gaye, Tammi Terrell, and Diana Ross? I have been told that I am a young man with an old soul. Just ask my spouse and she will quickly confirm this with a look of annoyance in her eyes since she considers herself a millennial.

I couldn't help but think about this song when I picked my mom up from the airport for a weeklong visit. This was my mother's first time on an airplane in her entire life. But when it comes to seeing her most recent granddaughter, I guess it's safe to say that there ain't no mountain high enough. There she was standing in the airport pick-up area with her Texas shaped carry-on bag smiling from ear to ear. You would've thought that my mom had been a jet setter her entire life.

In the Oliver household, when it comes to Journey, change is always on the horizon. This week, daylight savings time could not have come at a better time. We have been recently trying to figure out how to lengthen Journey's nightly sleep. So since Mother Nature encouraged us to spring forward, it has all worked itself out perfectly. Journey is also now sleeping in her crib and is nearly completely unswaddled. It is amazing to look at my daughter rolling around in her crib trying to find her a comfortable spot to fall asleep. I can only imagine what I must look like as an adult. She literally looks like she is possessed. One moment she's on one side of the crib and an hour later she has turned completely sideways. As my wife and I stare at the baby monitor we can't help but scratch our heads, smile, and relish in the joy in the journey.

Lesson 26

Transition

Tran•si•tion: noun

1. The process of growth that joins one phase of development with the next.

2. A passage of time; more qualitative and quantitative change.

Journey will be six months old later this week, and we are in a major transition phase of development. Up until this point, Journey has lived off of her mother's breast milk, but now we are starting to introduce her to solid foods. This is an exciting milestone that can be done in a few different ways. Some people start immediately with pureed fruits or vegetables. We started out with rice cereal. We mixed 2 tablespoons of rice cereal with 1 ounce of breast milk and right now, we are feeding this to Journey three times a day. We make sure that Journey doesn't have rice cereal during her last bottle-feeding of the evening because we don't want her to choke while she is sleeping from any fine-grained cereal that she doesn't swallow completely. We plan on moving on to pureed carrots and peas soon.

My spouse and I were beaming with excitement when we began to feed her rice cereal during our family breakfast this past weekend. For the past several weeks, Journey has been moving her mouth whenever she sees us eating. Her sweet little face had a moment of confusion as her baby spoon began to approach her mouth. Her mother held the baby spoon smiling from ear to ear as I moved my mouth back-and-forth mimicking eating something. All the attention was focused on Journey as the first few spoonfuls were filled with smiles and coos as the rice cereal dribbled down her cute little chin and onto her baby bib. Slowly she began to get the hang of it. A few things have changed since she has been eating rice cereal the past few days. She seems to be sleeping better as a couple of times she has gone to bed at 8:30pm and slept until 7:00 am, allowing my wife and I to sleep like champions. A few of her naps have been longer as well. She is also beginning to learn slowly but surely that by fussing or crying that she is able to influence how we as parents respond to her. For example, if she wants to be held, then she will begin to fuss and make

sounds as if she's trying to cough and laugh at the same time. But probably the most surprising change of all is that her poop is beginning to have a scent of its own. Like I said, things are *really* transitioning.

The other day, our friend and babysitter came over for dinner. Over the course of our conversations, our babysitter mentioned a couple named Gary & Anne Marie Ezzo. They specialize in childhood development. We purchased material from their website, Growingfamilies.com to help us understand the different stages of development that Journey will go through. We bought a book and DVD entitled, *The Babyhood Transitions: Parenting Your 5 to 12 Month Old.* Journey has also started to become a

little more mobile and is desperately trying to crawl. She just happens to spend more time pushing herself backwards than actually crawling forward. I imagine that in no time at all she will be running around the living room.

We have many more milestones and transitions to come with Journey and we are trying to be the best parents we can be. We are blessed to have her in our lives and we look forward to continuing to watch her grow and flourish.

Lesson 27

6-Month Check-Up

Journey had her six-month check-up this Monday and praise God, she is a healthy baby developing nicely. To quote the handout that was given to us she looks to have a "bright future." We did have a few questions that we wanted to make sure to get answered before we left the office:

- Can we go jogging with her? (obviously in a jogging stroller)

- What's the best way to handle constipation?

- Is it OK to start swimming lessons?

- Should we start giving her water?

We were told that it would be great to purchase a jogging stroller and start jogging with her. In fact, the doctor told us Journey would probably love it. So we purchased a Bob jogging stroller. This would also make sure that I didn't let that stay-at-home dad weight creep up on me.

We knew the answer before we asked the question, so we felt reassured when we were told an increase in liquid would help Journey with her recent constipation. We had recently added puréed carrots to Journey's feeding time, but I didn't do the best job setting her up for success. As a family, we went over to a friend's house during Easter weekend. Journey was distracted and did not fully finish her bottle. The next day, we went to church on Easter. Journey was distracted again during church and didn't fully finish that bottle. This is probably what led her to become constipated since she did not have enough liquids in conjunction with her puréed carrots. This led us to ask the question (much to my mom's excitement) if it was OK to give her water. We were told yes, just not in the replacement of her actual breast milk.

With excitement written all over my face due to the possibility being able to bond with Journey in a new way, I asked the doctor if it was OK to start swim lessons at the local YMCA. My spouse wasn't at the six-month check-up, but she was listening on speakerphone and I could feel her face light up with a smile as the doctor gave me a firm, "No." We may be going to the Caribbean in the fall for a family vacation and in my mind and imagination I had already pictured Journey swimming with the skills of a mermaid. Journey's doctor, however, brought me back to reality by saying she didn't see any benefit to teaching a baby how to swim until they were at least two to three years old. She said the whole experience is quite terrifying for them when their head is dunked under water. She went on to say it's OK to have them play in water, but the experience of trying to learn how to swim at this stage is probably not very beneficial for a baby. Not wanting to completely relinquish the possibility of having Journey try out for the Olympics, I asked the doctor how many kids she had and when did they learn how to swim. Knowing that my wife was still listening on speakerphone and was now probably jumping up-and-down with excitement, the doctor put the conversation completely to bed. She went on to tell me that she has three kids and all of them did not learn how to swim until they were three years old. I know when to admit that I have lost the battle and this one was definitely a loss. I'll revisit the conversation in about two and half years.

Journey is in the 93rd percentile for her height. She is right on par with every area and stage she should be in at this moment. She feeds well, we are slowly introducing new foods, and our family and friends are a good source of support. Her teeth should be starting to come in at any moment, her development continues to grow as we read and play with her, she likes her crib, and we are beginning to become even more aware of her safety as she picks everything up and stuffs it in her mouth. If things continue on this track, we won't be seeing Journey's doctor again until she is nine months old. Overall, we are truly blessed and it is an absolute joy to continue on this journey.

Lesson 28

Vacation

I have often heard people say absence makes the heart grow fonder. My spouse and I took our first vacation together this past week without our daughter Journey. My mother-in-law came into town the day before we left for vacation to get settled in to watch after our baby girl. From the moment I picked my mother-in-law up at the airport, I was like an eager kid the day before his birthday. I was filled with excitement and relaxation because I knew for the next four days, I was going to be relieved of my stay-at-home dad duties.

It was that I felt I deserved or was an entitled to a vacation—I was simply exhausted and I needed a vacation to get recharged. Before I became a stay-at-home dad, I used to speak for a nonprofit organization called Rachel's Challenge. That company allowed me to touch people's lives and I was on the road sometimes up to 250 days a year. It wasn't unusual for me to have a dozen flights in a week. So as I checked in at the airport, I felt like I was seeing a familiar friend. I'm that weird guy that loves everything about traveling, from packing up my bag, to speaking to random people, to managing the stress of delayed flights—I love it all; I love the hustle and bustle.

It also dawned on me that this was our first vacation together since my wife was six months pregnant. So it had been right at a year since the last time we had gone somewhere together for an extended stay. I was looking forward to the opportunity to not only recharge, but more importantly, to reconnect. I knew our daughter was in completely good hands with my mother-in-law.

We couldn't think of a better place to unwind than Napa Valley, California. As I tasted my first glass of wine and began to soak in the gorgeous

Napa Valley views, I quickly realized that this wasn't going to be like any other vacation I had experienced. In fact, this wasn't going to be like any other vacation my spouse and I had experienced together. As much fun as we were having and as much as we enjoyed reconnecting, Journey was never far from our thoughts. My wife would check in with my mother-in-law periodically, and my mother-in-law did a great job updating us with beautiful pictures of Journey. But nothing could replace holding our daughter close and feeling her soft skin. I missed playing with her toes when giving her a bottle and nibbling on her ears before kissing her cheeks.

I slept like a baby knowing I did not have to wake up until I was ready. I relished in the adult conversations I was having with people who were actually able to talk back(Journey isn't quite there yet). As I boarded a plane to return home from recharging and reconnecting, I realized no matter how much fun I had on vacation, I never felt complete. I always felt like something was off, like something was missing. It wasn't until I was back at home and were both hugging and kissing Journey that I felt completely whole again. Because in that moment, I had the two most important things in my life: my girls.

Lesson 29

Prince

The Day The Music Died. On the 3rd of Feb 1959, 22-year-old Buddy Holly, the Big Bopper, and Ritchie Valens, aged 17, died in a plane crash shortly after takeoff from Clear Lake, Iowa. For many people who grew up during this era, music for them would no longer be the same. I wouldn't be born until 20 years later so I have no idea about the magic I missed if I could have seen one of these rock stars in concert. If it wasn't for the movie La Bamba, I truly couldn't even tell you with the slightest idea anything about Ritchie Valens. It's not that I don't have an appreciation for music, I just don't know what I missed.

When Michael Jackson died in 2009, I was saddened like most people in the world, and when Whitney Houston died in 2012 I was saddened once again. But when Prince Rogers Nelson died on April 21, 2016, I went into mourning and finally got the meaning "The Day The Music Died." What added to my grieving was that I can say I had the amazing honor and pleasure of seeing Prince live in concert at the Toyota Center in Houston on August 7, 2004. We even had a black and white Shih Tzu for 11 years who's name was Prince. He too was cremated after he died four years ago from heart disease. Now his ashes are in a pine book with a gold label "Prince" in our living room. But now after having my daughter, Journey his death saddens me even more because she will never know who Prince was. Yes, she can listen to his many albums and watch his cult classic Purple Rain, however it's not the same as being able to see him walk out onto a stage.

I guess this is a feeling all parents have when they want to share a part of their childhood with their own children. I know this is true for me. There are a number of people who are considered the "greatest of all time" by many. Take for instance Dads who grew up watching running backs Jim Brown or Walter Payton (as for me, it was Barry Sanders and Emmitt Smith). My basketball greats were Magic Johnson and Michael Jordan. Golf for me was Tiger Woods and Greg Norman. Baseball, there was Barry Bonds and Derek Jeter. There are so many different categories: actors, actresses, cars, cities, beaches, food, movies, and so on. Oprah stands alone. I don't know who will be the greats of Journey's generation. I don't doubt we will have our chances to bond over few. But nothing will ever compare to Prince.

Lesson 30

Re-established

Before my spouse and I left for our vacation, we read a book and watched a DVD informing us that it would take a little time to get Journey re-established to her routine. It said that for however long Journey is out of routine, it would take her about half that amount of time to get re-established. This would be true even if we're traveling during the holidays as an entire family or if Journey goes to grandma's house for a few days. Basically, anything that will cause her to be disconnected from her normal, structured routine for a certain amount of time will cause her to be off.

Our vacation lasted four days. I have to often remind myself that this is my mother-in-law's only grandchild. As much as she does to try to stay consistent to the schedule my spouse and I have developed, it's never quite the same as if Mom and Dad were enforcing it. So, I have already mentally made the proper adjustments knowing that Journey is going to be spoiled when she spends time with her grandmothers. This is what they are supposed to do. I also know that I'm going to have to be twice as patient while our family works to get back into the swing of things.

Before we left for vacation, Journey was sleeping from 8:30 pm to 7 am. If she happened to wake up, it was typically around 6:00 am to 6:30am and she would typically put herself back to sleep. Before we left to go on vacation, I knew that my mother-in-law was going to sleep in the same room with Journey, so it did not shock my spouse and me that this was one of the first things she told us when we got home. In the short time we were gone Journey had gotten comfortable having her grandmother sleeping in the same room with her and comforting her immediately when she made the slightest fuss. It goes without saying that I was awakened from a very deep sleep when my sweet little baby girl starting crying at 4:30 am in the morning our first night back from vacation.

By the second night, Journey slept until 5:45 AM and after about 10 minutes of fussing and no one picking her up, she realized that her grandmother was no longer in the room with her. So she put herself back to sleep and did not wake up until 7 AM. Getting her back on track with her naps was not as difficult as I thought it was going to be. Within the first day back from vacation, she took a couple one-hour naps and one nap for a solid two hours. For me the key is always about being mentally prepared. I can't say I'm always going to have the information necessary in order to anticipate what's going to happen next, but if I can mentally have some type of preparation, it helps me in dealing with change. The great thing is that my spouse and I have used the tools and have seen them work before. We just need to get back to the basics as quickly as possible and get her back on her schedule. She's a happier baby for it!

Lesson 31

Are you a stay-at-home dad?

I've heard the song One is the Loneliest Number ever seen. It sounds like a pretty cool song, but to experience it is quite a different story. There have literally been times when I have been leaving the grocery store and have seen another man pushing a basket with the baby inside, and with my daughter and groceries still in the basket I have run across three parking lanes to run down that guy and ask him if he's a stay-at-home dad. After the initial shock of *where did you come from* expression on their face I am usually given the response of "No" with a scoff and the added "I'm just off from work today, but I wish I was." This is when I disappointingly respond that I'm just looking for some friends for my daughter and me. Slowly, I turn around and push our basket full of groceries to the truck.

I would be happy with just one stay-at-home dad friend. Most days if the weather permits, Journey and I go for a nice stroll in the park, sometimes up to 4 miles. It's not unusual for us to cross paths with a half a dozen moms pushing their kids in strollers. Most of them seem to always have at least one other person with them enjoying a delightful conversation. As the weather is becoming nicer and spring is here, I once saw a group of mothers with their young infants and toddlers enjoying an afternoon picnic. If we are lucky, Journey and I will be graced with a smile or a wave, but that's about it.

When I do any type of research to learn more about the development of my daughter, I have not seen any information directed at a stay-at-home—it's as if the general assumption that dads are sitting on the sidelines holding down the bench rather than nurturing the child. There have been those particular moments when an elderly woman in the grocery store, my doctor during my annual check-up, the cashier at Sprouts, or a flight attendant says, "I think it's amazing that you are a stay at home dad. You will never know the impact that you will have in your daughter's life by being there." I know that they are right. My bride, mom, mother-in-law, brothers, and family friends have all said that they think I am doing an awesome job, and I am grateful to know that they notice. However, I would love to hang around with a group of stay-at-home dads and share stories that are unique to our experiences. Trust me when I say that I can tell you what's going on in Journey's life better than I can tell you about what's happening in my life most of the time. I'm not saying this in an arrogant or cocky way. It's just natural, given the amount of time we spend together and how I study her. And for this, I am truly grateful. I understand that this is the greatest opportunity, blessing, responsibility, duty, job, career, and honor to be a father to my daughter Journey that all starts with me being a loving husband to her mother and my bride first.

Are you a stay at home dad?

Lesson 32

Wheels Up

Before I became a stay-at-home dad, I would travel about 250 days a year as a professional speaker. I did that for 6 years and I was constantly on the move. It wasn't unusual for me to have 4 flights in a day or stay in 4 different hotel rooms in a week. There were times when I felt frustrated when dealing with delayed flights or sometimes driving a rental car the size of a Prius because this was all that was available. For a 6'3 ½ and 230-pound guy, that's a tight squeeze. However, I will admit that I am one of those rare geeky breeds that really truly enjoys traveling. From packing my luggage, to talking with random travelers along my trip, I find it pretty enjoyable. One of the things I would often do before taking off on a plane is call my mom and tell her that I loved her. Then I would talk with Saran before the plane took off and send her a text before shutting off my phone.

One of the great things about my wife is that she equally enjoys traveling. She doesn't necessarily enjoy flying, but she has always described it as a necessary evil to get to where she's trying to go. So, it works very well for the both of us because we are always anticipating our next trip. We actually have a little family saying that when we are moving, hustling, bustling and things begin to feel a little overwhelming, we call it "team too much" to help us come back to reality. This tells us that we have too much going on at one time and we need to reassess the situation.

This past weekend was a "team too much" kind of a weekend. One of the reasons that we named our daughter Journey is because of the fact that we truly enjoy traveling. So this past weekend, Journey earned her namesake by taking her first plane ride. Out of all my experiences of flying, I have always wondered how it would be the first time my child rides on an airplane. Most of the babies I've ever seen on a plane haven't really enjoyed it as much as I have. The altitude and cabin pressure of the airplane really causes a lot of discomfort for a baby's ears, and this was a fear I had for Journey.

There were a couple of major things that were happening that kicked this whole trip off. First, my wife is a huge Beyoncé fan and she was performing in Houston that weekend. On top of that, it was Mother's Day weekend. So, what better way to enjoy your first Mother's Day weekend than to fly back to Texas to see your friends, family, and Beyoncé. Lucky for us, we were flying United Airways who allowed us to check our baby car seat for free. We also had Amazon deliver a new pack and play to my mother-in-law's house. The main goal was to try to eliminate as many extra pieces of luggage as possible. Also, I saved a video on YouTube to help me install the car seat base in the rental car in case I had any problems re-installing it. We decided not to take a stroller and instead my wife carried Journey in a hands free wearable baby carrier. Since Journey loves to kick off her socks and shoes, we put a pair of pants on her that have the feet attached to them so we wouldn't have to worry about her feet getting dirty in the airport or losing her socks and shoes.

Once we gathered our luggage together, we only had to pay for one checked bag. We proceeded to the TSA checkpoint and this is when we were quickly told that we needed to go back to the United check-in counter and have them add an infant notification for Journey onto one of our tickets. Once we went back going through, TSA was no problem. My wife did have a slight issue with her breast milk and breast pump but it was nothing major, just a little extra screening.

After getting settled into our seats on the plane, we began giving her a bottle as the plane took off in order to time it with her feeding schedule. The entire flight after Journey finished her bottle could not have gone any better. For all she knew, she could have been riding down the road in a car while sitting shotgun. She was absolutely perfect—not one fuss, in fact, she laughed and giggled and played the entire trip.

Beyoncé was amazing as always and Saran had a beautiful first Mother's Day with family and friends. She enjoyed the gift that I got her and the attention to detail that I went through to make it a special day. On our return flight back home, Journey had another stellar repeat performance as a great traveler. I am not naïve enough to think that is going to always be like this, however for her first time ever on an airplane as a family, I could not be happier. Despite it being a "team too much" weekend, we pulled everything off well.

Lesson 33

First Words

I can imagine that for some parents, anticipating the first words their child will ever say is like sitting at the Oscars waiting for your name to be read for winning Best Actor or Best Actress—*And the winner is"*…

For me, it has been a far different experience. I spend the majority of my time reading to and speaking with Journey. For months now, Journey has been babbling with greater diversity, making new sound combinations and intonations. She tries to imitate my speech with phrases like "bah-BAH-bah" or "dah-dah-dah." I have pretend conversations with her and we take turns "talking."

Things took a slight turn Monday morning as I was giving her a breakfast bottle. I began to really focus on mouthing and saying the word "mama" while Journey was enjoying her bottle. She stopped and began to press her lips together and move her jaws in the same way that I was moving mine to say the word "mama." Then my ears heard the sweetest little voice in world say, "mama."

Just to make sure that I wasn't just hearing things, I started the process all over again and she continued saying mama. While my wife was getting ready for work, I took the opportunity to videotape Journey saying her first words with my iPhone. I sent it to Saran, and it goes without saying, she lit up like a Christmas tree. The real winner is Journey because she could actually understand and mimic exactly what I was doing. I am truly amazed at God's creation. I know that it is only be a matter time before the celebration of hearing her first words will be replaced with, "Shh, Journey, be quiet and go to bed"; but for now, hearing her first words is sweet music to our ears.

Lesson 34

Childproof

"Parents worry endlessly about how to protect their children from stranger abduction and violence, but many overlook one of the biggest threats to their children's safety and well-being — their own home. Experts say that children between the ages of 1 and 4 are more likely to be killed by fire, burns, drowning, choking, poisoning, or falls than by a stranger's violence."-BabyCenter

Journey is eager to become Daddy's little helper. Over the last couple of weeks, she has quickly gotten better at maneuvering her little walker. It is so cool to see her little brain working on how to connect the puzzle pieces when it comes to backing up or moving forward. She has gone from bumping into kitchen cabinets to learning how to back up and make a 180° turn. If I go from the center of our kitchen to our breakfast nook, she is able to make the corner and identify exactly how to get to where I'm standing.

So with her quick little feet and developing brain, she is constantly on the move when she is in her walker. This means that I constantly need to be aware of where she is and what objects may be a hazard. My wife and I typically keep a tiny dry erase board on the front of the dishwasher to communicate if the dishes in the dishwasher are clean or dirty. Well, Journey is now able to work herself over to the board and take the dry erase marker from its clip holder and the first place she wants to put the marker is in her mouth.

Just the other day, I was taking dishes out of the dishwasher and Journey whipped around in her little walker and made a beeline for the dishwasher. The first thing she reached for was the knives! As I grabbed her tiny little hands, I told her that the knives were sharp and one day she will be able to help Daddy with the dishwasher, just not today.

I also have to make sure that the carpet is clean and free from any type of tiny objects that Journey could accidentally swallow or choke on. Journey was rolling around on the floor in her bedroom playing while I was changing the sheet on her mattress the other morning, when I noticed that she had a shiny little button in her hand. I have no idea how she got it but I know it's the same little sticky buttons we have used to decorate a tiny chalkboard in her room.

I recently read the best safety tip is to baby proof before you need to do. Your home—you know it well, but no one knows it better than your baby will. Your curious little one will discover, probe, and test every nook and cranny. Even if you've read the books, gotten advice from everyone you know, and then taken all the precautions you can think of, dangers lurk beyond what your eyes easily see. How do you make sure everything is safe and sound? Some parents seek the help of an expert.

This is a very in-depth topic with so many different layers. There are programs called Safe and Sound and Gadgets Galore. Other things to do include: protecting outlets, using caution with furniture and fixtures, installing gates, checking ties on blinds and curtains, and securing your windows and doors. The overall goal is to prevent poisoning, drowning, fires, and to prepare for an emergency. As we continue this journey together, I will be revisiting this topic along the way while trusting and praying that God will keep His protected hands on Journey's health and safety.

Lesson 35

You Gotta Crawl Before You Can Walk

"You gotta crawl before you can walk" is a saying that I have been familiar with for quite some time. I can't remember the first time I ever heard it—maybe when I was a young child or teenager, but I definitely know I've heard it once or twice as an adult. If you were to Google the saying, "You gotta crawl before you can walk" here are a few of the explanations you would read:

-You have to learn the basics first.

-You have to start a bit at a time.

-You can't get ahead of yourself

-You have to make sure that you achieve things before saying you are going to and sometimes you might not get there.

Sometimes it literally means that you must learn to move on your hands and knees before learning to walk. As a baby, you learn how to crawl, first before you walk; it's just a life cycle. With anything new, it will take time before you are really good at it. You have to take baby steps toward learning something new, and sometimes you have to take a smaller step before you can take a larger step.

Well, Journey turned eight months this past Friday and by Saturday afternoon, she began slightly crawling and finally by Sunday mid day she was an expert. So much so that she began to even pull herself up on things that she could reach when she got to her destination. My wife and I had to take a family trip to Babies R Us to get an extra large baby gate to help keep her in a safe area while crawling in our living room.

It goes without saying that this is a game changer for sure. It's very exciting, but I am thankful to God for the awareness that each little milestone she reaches also affirms that she isn't going to be a baby forever. We all have to grow up eventually. As happy as I am to see the advancements that she is achieving, a part of me feels a little sad. One of the goals for me is to stay in the moment. Sometimes I can get so far ahead of myself that I'm already preparing for the next stage of her life without enjoying the one that she is presently living in. It really does go by pretty fast, and before long, she will be running into her first day of class. With the awareness that I have been given, I want to absorb as many precious moments that I can carry in my heart and soul of this joy in the journey.

Lesson 36

Is that my daughter?

I can imagine that over the course of any parent's life, they will step back and ask themselves the question, "Is that my child?" Usually this question comes up when the child has done something great or something ridiculously weird. It can be interpreted as a sense of pride or embarrassment. The question may be followed by a gesture of come and give me a hug or a downward headshake expressing your disbelief at what they've done.

After a long and much-needed week vacation in Jamaica relaxing, reconnecting, rekindling, and rejuvenating with my bride, we returned home. My mother-in-law, without any persuasion, wanted to relish the time with her granddaughter, so she was gracious enough to take care of Journey while we were on vacation. As I walked into our home, I tossed my keys on the counter and ran towards my sweet little daughter. I fell on the carpet and began to open my arms anticipating her crawling towards me. As she began to approach me, I quickly noticed how much she had changed in just a week. I thought to myself, "Is this my daughter?" She looked taller and her face looked fuller. She had this new motion that she would do with her mouth as if she were attempting to stick out her tongue, but instead, she would just push the tip of her tongue past her lips. I know what you're thinking, *how could you notice all that in that brief moment?* The truth is I don't know how I did, I just did.

I began to beam with a love that only a father can have for their child. Journey stopped halfway during her crawling as if to inspect and make sure I was the person she thought I was. I already knew from a previous trip that she wasn't going to immediately melt like butter in my arms. With her mom and grandmother being there, she paused to scan the room and collect the other faces. I met her halfway and wrapped her up in my arms and it felt so great to smell her and feel her soft skin. In just a week, she had grown and developed in such an extraordinary and beautiful way. To think that this happens before my very eyes on a daily basis and I can sometimes miss it is crazy.

Despite all the love and joy it brought me to hold Journey once again, I know that there will be times when I will be disappointed in Journey maybe because of her actions, behaviors, or attitudes. Nevertheless, I pray that God fills my heart with the same amount of grace that He has shown me when I have caused Him to question if I was His child. I get so excited when I see the changes taking place in Journey's life because it's like a gift that keeps on giving. It keeps me on the edge of my seat wondering and curious about what is going to happen next.

Lesson 37

My First Father's Day

F: faithful, forgiving

A: admiring, attentive

T: true, trustworthy

H: honoring, heroic

E: encouraging, enduring

R: responsible, respected

You embody all these attributes and more. Journey is so very blessed to have you as a father. Regardless of the sins of our fathers, you have stepped up and exemplified what it means to be a man, husband, and father.

Be on your guard; Stand firm in the faith; Be courageous; Be strong- 1 Corinthians 16:13

That is the message I received in my first Father's Day card from my wife and almost 9-month-old daughter, Journey. Reading this card was so humbling. The reason being is one of my character defects is that I am a perfectionist, and to make things worse, I want things done on my terms. There have been many times in this first year being a father that I have felt like I wasn't good enough or doing enough. I have even judged myself for being a stay-at-home dad at times feeling like I need to do more and be bigger and better because society thinks this isn't a man's role. I've even had family members tell me that I need to get a real job. So when I reached down to pick Journey up from her crib on Father's Day morning

I whispered to her that having her puts me in an entirely new status with a completely new title. I told her 'thank you' for blessing me to become her father. God made me for this role.

It just so happened that during this past week, I had my thirteen-year-old niece and two eleven-year-old twin nephews in town. It had been camp Oliver for sure with 3 kids, an 8 month old, two dogs, and a cat. This caused my wife and I to laugh out loud when she took me to a nice steakhouse brunch for Father's Day and the manager gave us a free round of mimosas. I think he thought poor woman with four kids having to deal with this guy on Father's Day; hopefully this will liven up their day.

I did find it a little uncomfortable to hear "Happy Father's Day" from strangers and via texts and phone calls from family and friends. A small part of me felt like there was more I needed to do, like I hadn't earned it yet. Then I remembered some wisdom that one of my mentors gave me over twelve years ago. He simply said when someone says something nice to you the best response you can give him or her in return is "thank you."

As the day came to a close, I looked at a picture that my wife put up on Facebook of our little family. The three of us looked radiant as if we were truly reflecting the goodness of God in our lives. It felt weird looking at this beautiful picture because I just couldn't believe that this was actually my family. I was once again filled with humility. All I could say over and over again was thank you Jesus for my family. My wife showered me with gifts and love. My daughter covered me with kisses and love. My niece and nephews spoke with kind words. I couldn't ask or pray for a better day. It was beautiful.

Lesson 38

9 Months

Remember, your baby is an individual. All babies are unique and meet milestones at their own pace. Developmental guidelines simply show what your baby has the potential to accomplish — if not right now, then soon. If your baby was premature, keep in mind that kids born early usually need a bit more time to meet their milestones. If you have any questions at all about your baby's development, ask your healthcare provider.-Baby Center

Being a parent, particularly a stay-at-home dad, one of the common pitfalls I try to avoid is the comparison game. Where is Journey on her development skills and how is she doing compared to other babies? Although I struggled to learn this as a child, as an adult, I know that nothing good comes out of comparing myself to others; all you get is envy, jealousy, and coveting which only leads to self-doubt, judgment, and shame.

We have a saying in the Oliver family: "Stay in your lane." This is what my wife and I say to one another when we find ourselves comparing ourselves to others and society. One of my very good accountability brothers sometimes gently reminds me when he sees me slipping into comparing myself by saying, "God has you right where you are supposed to be." All of this is important to remember as Journey rounds the corner into her ninth month of life. It's not fair to my little girl to place her above or below anyone else. I don't want my attitude or behavior to appear as if I am judging, being envious, jealous, or coveting another baby or parents based off where Journey is in her life.

"We may compare ourselves to those we call 'normal.' Such comparisons are pointless, however. It's human to look for similarities between ourselves and others; we all search for connection; but it's freeing to realize that each of us is unique. Some people are healthier than we are, and some people are sicker. Neither state need reflect on us, because each of us is where we're supposed to be."--Answers in the Heart.

I could go down an endless path of comparing the different areas of the development of Journey other babies. Constant comparisons, however, can lead to the type of parenting where I place perfection over everything else causing Journey to grow up never feeling good enough. It may seem like a little thing, but my college football coach used to tell us, "If you take care of the little things, the big things will take care of themselves." So if I keep this mindset of being aware of my comparisons now, I can avoid making a fool out of myself when Journey gets older and she starts participating in this thing we call life.

Lesson 39

I'm No Role Model

I remember growing up watching a series of commercials with the NBA Hall of Famer Charles Barkley talking about why it wasn't his job to be a role model for other people's children. I was so young that I didn't understand why parents were getting so upset with Sir Charles Barkley. I heard many parents discussing why it was wrong for Barkley to have the attitude that he did. When I became older and began to experience life a little bit more for myself, I sort of understood the parents' perspectives. Because Barkley had the platforms of the NBA and the media, he was highly visible and could impact children's lives by being a positive role model. However, after now having my own child, I understand his perspective a lot better and his original point of view makes more sense to me. Being a role model to children—for me, specifically being a role model to Journey—starts at home, not in the community or among celebrities or athletes.

After seeing our doctor for Journey's 9-month check-up, she gave me a handout to take home with me. While reading it over, I reached the section entitled "Your baby and family." One of the bullet points said "Do things the way you want your baby to do them-you are your babies role model." I have already noticed that whatever I am doing, Journey wants to do the same thing. I have also noticed that there are two things that I often have in my hand. One is my cell phone and the other is the remote control. So it's not a surprise that most of the time, Journey is either reaching for my cell phone or the remote control. It's not that she knows what they are and what they do, but it's that she is thinking, "If this thing requires so much attention from my dad, then I want to check it out and see what it is myself."

There are some fun games and activities that I can model for Journey. For example, when I am cooking in the kitchen I can give her a small measuring cup to play with and help her feel as if she is helping Daddy cook. When I am using fruits and vegetables, I can show them to her and let her touch them while explaining to her what they are and how they can be used. Also, when I am communicating with my bride, I can be an example of showing her a healthy way to communicate. It always makes me smile when I give my spouse a long hug and a kiss to look back over my shoulder and see Journey smiling at the both of us.

The important area of Journey's life that I can influence by being a good role model is being obedient, having a God-fearing relationship with Jesus, and honoring my wife by the way that I love her and show her respect. I won't do this perfectly but I'd rather place the challenge in my hands then leave it up to society. Yes, it takes a village, but the buck starts here.

Lesson 40

Expressions

Journey is starting to express her emotions in more complex ways – shaking her head in refusal when she doesn't want any more of her bottle, preferring her mother over anyone else, and getting upset when Saran leaves the room. As Journey becomes more social, she'll keep expanding her repertoire of tricks to include clapping, waving bye-bye, pointing to what she wants or to show me something she finds interesting, shrieking to attract my attention, laughing at silly sounds and expressions, and using a specific cry to convey a particular "request."

My mom is in town visiting for a week to spend time with Journey. The other morning, I overheard her reading *The Three Little Pigs* to Journey. As I began to listen more closely, I chuckled to myself because Journey was speaking and expressing herself by babbling and jabbering after each word my mother read out loud as if *she* were reading *The Three Little Pigs* to her grandmother and not the other way around.

The torrent of words Journey has been hearing since birth is beginning to work its magic, although her understanding of words far outpaces her ability to use them. Her babbling has turned to jabber and is almost starting to sound a little like real words, phrases, and sentences. JoJo (our nickname for Journey) thinks she's saying something, so as a family we respond as if she really is!

At this point, Journey still comprehends more from my tone than from my actual words. This is why it is important that I don't overuse the word "no." I try to make it a point to only use a very firm tone while combined with the word "no" whenever she is in harms way. If not, she will just connect "no" with being just any other word. If I'm always firm or yelling, she will just consider that a natural way of speaking and not be able to make a distinction between the two. She can understand when I'm pleased. The more I talk to Journey-either directly or while doing other things, such as preparing dinner, driving, or getting dressed—the more she learns about communication and expressions.

Lesson 41

Take care of yourself

I honestly don't know how single parents do it. Being a first-time stay-at-home dad, I have a new found understanding of the role after 10 months on the job. Being Journey's dad and primary care giver is a 24 hours a day and 7 days a week responsibility. I will be the first to admit that if it weren't for my wife, I would've lost my sanity a long time ago. We make a great team and she does an exceptional job of bringing balance to my life.

We also have the added support of my mother-in-law and mom when they come into town to visit, and we also have two outstanding friends/alternate caregivers that have blessed us by taking care of Journey when we want some alone time together. Mixing all these people together, we have the foundation of a small village to raise a single child. However being with Journey the majority of the time day in and day out, I experience the newness she brings to my life on a regular basis.

There aren't many moments where she's not on my mind constantly. I'm always thinking about her: health, development, nap times, eating schedule, poop times, and safety. This constant amount of thinking, movement, and activity makes it very critical that I take care of myself physically, emotionally, spiritually, and mentally. If I'm not in a good place in these areas of my life, I'm not going to be able to be in a good place to properly take care of my daughter.

Here are some of the ways I go about taking care of myself:

- Getting to bed early- I'm typically in bed by <u>9:45 PM</u> and I'm normally asleep between <u>10:15-10:30 PM</u>. Regardless of what's going on in my life, Journey is still going to wake up between 6:00 and 7:00 AM.

- Naps, naps, naps- I try to take one nap daily. This is normally during Journeys second nap of the day, which is in the late afternoon. I typically try to nap anywhere from 10 to 30 minutes. It's not like I'm doing a lot of strenuous work, so most of the time I don't know that I'm actually tired. But that's a dangerous place to be because then I can get careless.

- Exercise- Monday, Wednesdays, and Fridays I wake up at 4:20 AM and I'm at my CrossFit gym by 5 AM for a one hour intense workout. Tuesdays and Thursdays I typically work out from home with some form of cardio and weights.

- In the Word- I spend time reading my Bible daily and praying daily. I make it a point to start my day off by spending time with God, then trying to make a conscious effort to remain connected with Him throughout the day. I also read a daily meditation devotion and I journal at least once or twice a week.

- Accountability team- I have a group of men that I check in with daily to stay accountable in all areas of my life. These men help me stay authentic and in integrity. My ability to effectively guide and parent Journey is directly related to my own personal integrity. I also have several men that I mentor. I speak with at least one of them daily. This helps me feel like I have some adult connection. About once a week, one of my best friends named, Philip calls me to just talk. This helps me stay connected to current events and laughter.

- Unwind time- I have a PS4 and I normally will play it at least once during the weekend. Whenever my mother-in-law or mom is in town, I try to go out at least twice a week to play golf or hit balls.

- Spousal connection- Twice a month Saran and I will have date night or do something nice for one another like take a hot bubble bath or drink some wine.

- Don't isolate- Once a day, I make it a point to get out of the house with Journey. It doesn't matter if we're going grocery shopping, for a walk, or to the post office. Getting out of the house and getting some fresh air is key to not isolating myself.

- Asking for help- My wife can't help me with what's going on in my life if I don't share it with her. So if there's anything I need, I make it a point to check in with her and ask for help.

Finally, my theme for this year is "less is more". So when I begin to feel like I'm getting overwhelmed or losing my sanity, God gently reminds me to slow down, take it easy—this too shall pass.

Those are the tools I use to take care of myself, but here are some other examples you may want to try out for yourself:

Practice a yoga pose, escape through reading, get a makeover, shop online, help someone out, take a bath (even if it's in the morning), or take a walk.

I don't go about taking care myself perfectly, so the good thing is I get to practice this as often as I want. The important thing to remember is taking care of myself helps me become a better parent for Journey.

Lesson 42

Weekend Getaway

My how times have changed. This could not be more accurate when it comes to weekend getaways. My bride and I were married for almost 6 years before we became pregnant with our daughter Journey. Until then, weekend getaways were full of romance, adventure, and spontaneity. The days leading up to our extended weekends of "quality time" would have me feeling like I was a newlywed again. I had an extra pep in my step, a smile that shined brighter than Christmas morning, and I would catch myself just day dreaming about my wife.

We were invited to attend one of our closest friend's family reunion in Memphis, Tennessee last weekend. This was our first getaway without any extra family support (i.e. grandparents). The days leading up to the trip took on a different form of planning since we are now parents. I went to have our dog's medical records updated with their current shots before dropping them off for boarding. We arranged to pick up a rental car because we realized there wouldn't be enough room in our Camry or Tacoma for all our stuff. I also made sure that our cat would have enough food and water as well as fresh litter in her box. Saran had arranged for us to stay at the Doubletree Hotel where the family reunion was being held to enjoy the festivities.

By 4 o'clock on Thursday afternoon, we had packed up all of our luggage plus a baby gate, a portable baby crib, baby bottles/baby food, a stroller, and an alphabet baby gym mat (yes probably too much, but oh well). No golf clubs, no lingerie, no fun adult stuff. The trip was going to take a total of 6 hours driving taking us through Fort Smith and Little Rock, Arkansas. It was a beautiful drive and Journey was awesome the entire trip. Saran and I were both tired as the three of us checked into the hotel at 11 PM. We got Journey set up for bed as usual, and we tried to eat some food we picked up. We took turns watching Journey as we took a shower and got ready to go to bed around midnight. Journey typically goes to bed around 7:45 PM so she was well passed her bedtime.

I was under the impression that since it was so passed her bedtime she would be ready to pass out. I began to let my mind wander to the fact that we were on a weekend getaway and I began to get full of exceptions, which is never a smart thing to do. The moment Saran went to lay Journey down in her crib beside our bed, Journey jumped up and began to fuss and cry and scream "Mama!" Being in a hotel room we didn't want to be rude and let Journey wake up the other guest near us so Saran picked her to get her to calmed down. For the next 4 hours we tried with earnest to get Journey to fall asleep in her crib, but it just wouldn't happen. She just would not sleep in her crib with us in the same room. Finally, she fell asleep between the both of us in bed but neither of us could sleep comfortably or soundly because we didn't want to accidentally roll on top of her. Needless to say this wasn't what I was anticipating.

I strongly considered leaving first thing Friday morning and returning home. I was pretty sure both of us couldn't handle another night like that. But we didn't want to miss out on the festivities of the family reunion and these were some of my wife's closets friends that I know she wanted to spend time with. So we tried to find a last minute condo so Journey could have her own room and went with AirBnB. We found a cute little duplex down the street from the hotel. That was one of the best decisions we could've made because the next night, JoJo slept in her own room and never made a peep. We slept better also. JoJo was even able to get in a few naps.

We had a great time in Memphis. We went to the Civil Rights Museum, which I highly recommend; it should be a requirement for all high schools in America. We ate ribs on Beale Street, played kickball with the family, and laughed until our hearts burst with joy. We saw old friends, met new friends, and even met a Joy in the Journey follower! I even took one for the team by going home early with JoJo after dinner so Saran could stay out and party with friends. It really was a great trip; just different from our couples getaways. But that is all part of the joy in the journey. I learned that traveling with children can be very tiring but overall very rewarding and blessed with memories. My how times have changed.

Lesson 43

The biggest baby in the house

This is going to come as a huge surprise to my wife that I am actually admitting this out loud, however, the both of us have known this for years, even before Journey was born. I am the biggest baby in the house when it comes to getting any slight cold or sickness of any kind. Throughout most of the year, I genuinely feel 100% healthy. So when I feel like I'm getting a cold or the "crud" like I did this week, I honestly feel under the weather.

Now, it doesn't help that my lovely bride is a cardiologist and she truly sees not only sick people, but also diseased people often. So my little itchy throat, stopped up head, or cough isn't really more than a bump on a pickle to her. I do have a tendency to overreact and exaggerate at times. Nevertheless, when I am feeling sick, I expect her to pump the breaks and whip out her bedside manner.

We have a house packed with many souls: My bride, our sweet daughter, Journey, our poodle, Queen, our cat, Kitty (Baily), our Yorkie, King, and myself. Journey trumps us all in every area at this stage in her life, especially when it comes to health. I fall somewhere towards the end of the pecking order between Queen and King. By God's grace, JoJo has been experiencing good health. As life happens, she will one day get sick. That's normal and healthy because it will give her a chance to strengthen her immune system. This is when I will know for sure there is a new sheriff in town and it isn't me. I have to stop and laugh at myself because my wife looks at me in a way that says, "Boy you ain't sick." But all I want is my orange juice, chicken noodle soup (Campbell's) with fresh chopped parsley, and maybe a hot toddy. Did I mention I was a little extravagant?

That's what happens when you have grown up with all brothers, three in total. Our mom must have known she wasn't really treating our cold, but more our inner child ego. My wife growing up as an only child and her mom being a registered nurse they stick to the mantra "Treat problem and kept it moving." I must applaud my bride because I don't make it easy on her, and me being a middle child comes with an entirely different set of feeling left out, self centeredness, people pleasing, and perfection-ist issues.

Reality is, Journey is the baby and just like the Nyquil commercial says, there are no sick days when it comes to being a parent and a stay-at-home day. So in the words of Chris Rock's old stand-up comedy routine: Shut up and take some Robitussin.

Lesson 44

Till Death Do Us Part

I shared in a previous column that I once heard a statement so empowering on YouTube that it is now written on my bathroom mirror to see every morning. The statement is, "If you live each day as if it was your last, someday most certainly you'll be right. If today was the last day of my life, would I want to do what I am about to do today?" After today's meeting with our attorneys, I felt that this statement was definitely fitting.

My bride and I started on the non-sexiest, but most responsible and essential process for our daughter, Journey today. It's call "estate planning" i.e. what happens when one of us dies or when both of us die. Laws vary from state to state and apparently when living in Oklahoma, it's not just as simple as writing a will.

Here are some bullet points the attorneys will be counseling and helping us establish:

- Joint Revocable Trust

- Memorandum Trust

- Pour-Over Will

- Durable Power of Attorney for Financial Decisions

- Durable Power of Attorney for Health Care

- Oklahoma Advance Directive for Health Care

- Full asset analysts for correct titling of your assets

- Written "Estate Funding Plan" to guide you in the correct titling of your assets

- Laminated wallet-size card with the name of your trust

- Conference with two witnesses and notary

Needless to say, the emotional person that I am, I left the meeting feeling slightly depressed. OK let's just be honest, depressed.

Our attorneys advised us to list three people per situation for our power of attorney (health wise, guardianship over Journey, and financially) in case Saran and I both were to die at the same time or were in a coma and couldn't make health or financial decisions for ourselves. We could list the same people for each area or it could be an array of people. The first choice is easy because it would be either my wife or me. Easy in the sense of it's the obvious choice, but devastating in the heartbreak of no longer being with my boo. It gets scarier when thinking about the both of us being gone and Journey being cared for by someone else. Not to be disrespectful, but we are her parents and no one would ever raise her the way we would. It's just the reality of the situation. I have no doubt they would do the absolute best job ever, but it wouldn't be in the same way as us as her mom and dad.

I have to acknowledge our realtor for putting us on this path. She gave us the kick in the butt that we needed to get this ball rolling. While sitting in the meeting and in a pile of paperwork as we reached hour number 2 of the discussion, I felt like my brain was fried. I realized why I had been putting this off for so long; there truly isn't anything exciting about it at all. While holding Journey in my arms and listening to Saran talk about our life insurance with the attorneys, I realized that other than praying for Journey to one day have a relationship with The Lord and Savior Jesus Christ, this was one of the most necessary meetings we have ever had in our lives.

What it boils down to is trusting and letting go of control. Trust that God is in control and it's going to work out according to His will and not mine. The reason I say this is when discussing with your spouse who those three people may be, it puts me in a very weird and uncomfortable position of trying to control the unknown. So instead I choose to focus on the joy in the journey. The joy of knowing I love my bride and daughter and they love me in return. If I live each day as if it were my last, someday most certainly I'll be right. If today was the last day of my life, would I want to do what I am about to do today? Yes!!!!

Lesson 45

Play Date

After months of trying to find a stay-at-home dad group, I eventually started reaching out to stay-at-home mom groups in the Tulsa/Owasso area. Much to our delight, we were allowed to join both a stay-at-home mom group in Owasso and a stay-at-home mom group in Tulsa.

So today journey attended her first play date in the park with the Tulsa stay-at-home mom group. It was about a 30-minute drive away from our home; that's one of the great things about moving from Texas: anything under a two-hour drive is considered a skip. I found myself having anxiety as I began to get Journey ready for a play date and I didn't know where these feelings came from. I just want to Journey to be accepted. I realized that I was putting expectations on myself so as not to come across as an incompetent as a stay-at-home dad: I didn't want to be late or not have the things that she could possibly need for a play date.

Lucky for me, Journey woke up from her nap about an hour before it was time for us to head out the door. So she was able to get her second bottle of the morning, and a package of vegetable. I begin to list things that she could possibly need for this play day—after all, how long does a play day even last? I packed her stroller, a blanket, some snacks, a little baby plastic bowl for her snacks, a bib, extra diapers, and an extra change of clothes. What does a 10-month-old little angle named, Journey wear on a cold, overcast day at the park with a possible slight chance of rain and still a chance for the sun to pop out? A white sundress, of course.

God has placed many men in my life with whom I can be very honest and candid. I spoke with one of my mentors as I drove to the play date, and I told him about my anxiety and needing to just let go and be in the moment. He advised me that feelings are just feelings nothing more or nothing less, and that I should not allow them to sabotage myself from enjoying the moment. He also advised me to be gentle with myself (it's funny how if not handled and accepted in a healthy way, my junk can rob me of my joy in the journey).

As we parked the truck and took everything out, I place Journeys sun hat on her had and we began our stroll into the park. I had to shut my brain off from all the stereotypes I had seen in movies about stay-at-home mom groups, about the hierarchy and judging of others. After all, the objective is to introduce my daughter to the opportunity to connect with other children in a social setting. Not people pleasing or comparing— nothing good ever comes from those experiences, just envy, jealousy, and self-doubt.

I approached the area that looked like a common meeting spot for most of the moms. It was a wooden ship that had plastic slides connected to it and children were enjoying themselves and laughing. I introduced Journey and myself to several of the moms. I placed Journey on the ground and we both stood beside one another. Journey took a card out of her mom's DNA, which is to assess a situation before joining in. As I exchanged conversations with the other moms, Journey begin to loosen up and relax. Before long, she was just another kid at the park with her dad. Out of the 15 or so kids, Journey was the second youngest and the oldest kid was getting ready to join preschool the next day.

Within minutes, I felt completely welcome. I learned a ton of information about different ways to stay connected to the group. From other play dates to when the story times will be starting in the fall to what websites to visit to learn about more up coming events. All of the moms were very engaging. It didn't hurt that my daughter looked absolutely gorgeous and her behavior was amazing so she made my job look a lot easier. I repeatedly thank all the moms for being so nice and welcoming. I also told them don't be surprised if you see us about once a week. I'm happy because as the fall approaches, I have a few new things to put on my calendar to help Journey continue to grow and develop.

Lesson 46

Texas Two-Step

When it comes to dancing, let's just say as a family, we pray Journey will get her moves from her mother. I'm the guy in the middle of the party dancing to an entirely different rhythm than everyone else. The good thing is, I'm going to have a great time regardless of if I can dance or not.

One of my closest buddies, Levi is so good at doing the Texas two-step that when he is dancing, he looks as smooth as an ice skater on ice. I imagine in my head when my wife and I are doing our version of the Texas two-step that I'm dancing just as good as Levi. But the truth is, I more likely resemble my daughter Journey as she takes her first few steps. I have dubbed it the JoJo Texas two-step. She walks two quick steps in a row then pauses to gather her balance and then takes two more steps before falling on her bottom were she says in the cutest little voice "oh oh."

The other day, she walked almost 10 whole steps before she fell on the ground and began to clap and giggle celebrating her achievement. That's definitely something she has taken from me. She's going to celebrate regardless if she's the only one doing it. On June 1st, Journey started crawling and a few days later, she was pulling herself up to standing. Now she is a few days away from turning 11 months and she is walking. My goodness these experiences are going by so fast!

School is starting all over the country. My Facebook newsfeed has been covered with friends showing their cute little angels all dressed up looking their best as they head back to school. I can only imagine how it won't be long until I am doing the same thing with my own little bundle of joy.

One of the interesting things I've observed about Journey is that as she is learning to walk, she is not focused on falling down. As soon as she falls down, she pops right back up again. She is completely living in the moment of experiencing something new. It is as if every time she falls down, she learns something new the moment her bottom touches the ground and she is eager to jump right back up and put it to use. Once back on her feet, if she took two steps before she fell, now she is more likely to take even more steps as she balances her way through the experience. So often I get so discouraged after I fall down that I just stay there out of fear that I might fall again. Or when I do get back up, I'm so timid and hesitant from falling down, that I do not apply the lessons life taught me in the fall. Instead, I'm too focused on getting back to where I fell and worrying every step of the way. This makes it harder for me to stay light on my feet and reach places in my life I have yearned to experience.

Ultimately, I know that Journey feels safe because she feels the presence of her father always nearby watching her every step. She knows that I'm never going to let her get so far out of my reach that I cannot catch her when she falls. I also need to remember that my heavenly Father is always within my reach and He will catch me when I fall during my own Texas two-step through life.

Lesson 47

Holding Down The Fort

Before I became a father and a stay-at-home dad, the idea of having the whole house to myself when my wife was out of town made me feel like I was back in college again. The entire time would be spent playing videos games, eating Popeye's chicken, drinking beer, staying up late, and sleeping in. Zero focus on anyone else other than my own selfish needs.

Last week, my bride went out of town for seven days to study for her cardiology boards at the Mayo Clinic in Rochester, Minnesota. The idea of being at home while she is out of town is no longer the same experience since becoming a father. Holding down the fort had nothing to do with playing videos, drinking beer, eating fried chicken, and definitely not sleeping in. It's more like being in bed around 9:30 PM, waking up at 6:00 AM and solely being 1000% focused on our daughter, Journey.

Normally when my wife comes home from work during the week I have a little bit of time to myself. Nothing major—maybe half an hour to just chill and relax. I make it a point to give Saran some time to bond with Journey. However when it's Journey and me by ourselves for an extended period, taking power naps are a necessity. Lately, Journey has been really enjoying going to the park and playing on the swings. Overall, it is a feeling of solitude and joy when I hold down the fort for my family. Unlike the college kid who was solely focused on himself, it feels good to be a responsible adult.

Putting myself in my wife's shoes, I can only imagine that it truly tugs at her heart to be away from her family for so long. After all, she wasn't on vacation, but instead listening to lectures 12 hours a day. It was good that she had the ability to FaceTime and see Journey's sweet little face at least once a day. Since Journey is mastering the ability to walk, she takes the phone from my hand and walks around the floor while scratching the surface of the phone as if she's waving to her mom. It's safe to say that as much as Mommy misses us, we also miss Mommy when she's gone. The other night, just to help the time go by, I cleaned both of our bathrooms from top to bottom after putting Journey down for bed. That's the last thing I ever thought I would be doing when having the house all to myself.

Lesson 48

Journey being Journey

There have been many times during the past 11 months of Journey's life when her mom and I have asked ourselves: "Why is she doing that?", "Is that normal?", or "Do you think she is ok?" The answer is usually yes.

Why does Journey arch her back and throw herself backward when she's upset? This didn't really start until she was around 9 months old. Simply put, she isn't able to control her body when experiencing her emotions. "Virtually all babies go through this phase," says Bob Sears, a pediatrician in San Clemente, California, and the author of many parenting books. He states, "So even though it's not safe for your child to launch herself backward out of your arms, she doesn't have enough control to stop herself." The only time this can sometimes become an issue with Journey is after she has eaten because this can cause her to vomit a little bit of a food. If her mother and I are in the process of passing Journey off between one another we both are extra careful in holding her because her quick movements could cause her to be accidentally dropped. Overall, according to babycenter.com, this is all very normal, "But if your child is like most, the back-arching sessions signal nothing more than your child's growing independence and signify that her emotional development is right on track. So brace yourself and hang on: This won't be the last time you'll have to remain calm as your child's temper flares out of control."

Why does Journey suddenly wake up crying in the middle of the night? At this stage in Journey's life, the sudden waking up can be attributed to two main factors. First, is separation anxiety and this typically occurs when one of us is out of the house for a considerable amount of time, like recently when my wife was out of town for a week studying for her cardiology boards. This also sometimes happens when Saran and I return after being on vacation. The next reason that this sometimes takes place is that Journey is teething or some other form of development maturity is taking place in our little sweetheart. According to babycenter. com, "It's very common for even the best sleepers to suddenly start having problems, whether it's trouble falling asleep at bedtime or abruptly waking up during the night. Starting at age 6 months, separation anxiety can cause babies to wake up crying more than once during the night. Don't be surprised if your anxious baby does this and wants only you – or only your partner. Other common causes of night waking in previously good sleepers include illness or a looming developmental leap. In those cases, there are a couple of things to try, in addition to treating the fever or throat or ear pain that's making your sick baby uncomfortable." We typically let Journey sooth herself back to sleep.

Finally, why is Journey stuck on wanting to drink her bathwater? Yes. According to pediatrician Tanya Remer Altmann, editor of *The Wonder Years: Helping Your Baby and Young Child Successfully Negotiate the Major Developmental Milestones*, many parents say that drinking bathwater fascinates their babies. Altmann recommends discouraging this behavior, but says you don't need to be too concerned about it. More than anything, Journey is just being Journey. It's not like we're going to allow her to drink any real serious amount. She mainly just wants to suck on her wet bath towel.

This is a great opportunity during bath time to teach Journey a new skill. "The bath can be the ideal place to teach your child to drink from a regular cup," says Altmann. Offer up filtered or cold water from the sink faucet and let your child practice sipping from something unbreakable. If he dribbles, it's one place where it really doesn't matter.

All of these questions that come to the surface when experiencing the life of our little girl are normal and they add to the joy that we continue to find while on this journey.

Lesson 49

Planning Journey's First Birthday

I can still remember the conversation I had with the lady who helped us set up the timeshare we were suckered into getting on our honeymoon seven and a half years ago in Kauai, Hawaii. She told us how she and her husband had just finished spending $1,000 on one of their children's first birthday celebration, which included a bounce house. She went on to tell us that this wasn't even considered over the top because Hawaiians always go all out for first birthdays. Just the other day while taking Journey to the swings, I met a young lady with her toddler son. We made small talk and in the course of our conversation, we came upon the topic of first birthdays. She told me that she went over her budget by 300%, which included not only a bounce house, but a petting zoo as well.

I have heard everything from kegs of beer being at a first birthday party to personalized individual cupcakes. If I ever met the lady from our honeymoon again, I would tell her that I don't think it's just Hawaiians that have a tendency to go over the top on first birthdays, but people in general.

As the days come closer to Journey's birthday on the 27th, I hope and pray we fall somewhere in the middle in the celebration. In our marriage, I am the more extravagant and high maintenance one, especially during the holidays, birthdays, and special occasions. Saran is a little more modest and conservative. She understands regardless of how much money we spend or fun we have, bills still need to be paid and we still need to be able to live after the confetti has fallen. I will admit, I am a little more worried about my mother-in-law. This is her first and only grandchild and knowing how big her New Year's Eve parties can get and the fact that it's at her house back in Texas, who knows what to expect. I know my wife is going to have her hands full trying to keep it all in perspective.

By doing a quick search on the web, you can find a lot of great ideas and themes to make it all very reasonable and enjoyable for both children and adults who may attend. We have already had invitations made (by made I mean Walgreens) and ordered Journey's one-year birthday outfit. On a slightly different note, I just made Journey's appointment for her one-year check-up for the 28th, which I've been told can be a little painful for the babies because she will receive multiple vaccines. For that reason alone, I couldn't have my little sweetheart getting shots on her birthday. Like I said, I can be a little high maintenance.

Lesson 50

Letter to my Daughter

Dear Journey,

Early on in the beginning of Mommy and Daddy's marriage, we decided as a couple that Daddy was going to stay home and take care of you, while Mommy pursued her career as a doctor. This isn't how all families are, but this is what works best for our family. Everything Mommy and Daddy do is done with the thought of how will this be best for you. We know you are not always going to agree or enjoy our decisions, but the question we are seeking to answer when we make those decisions is always how will this enrich Journey's faith, health, development, and over all life?

Being a stay-at-home dad has come with many different emotions and experiences. Daddy didn't know that this was going to be the most challenging responsibility and job he has ever had, but he also didn't know that it was going to be one of the greatest rewards and blessings of his entire life. Journey, I chose to write a column and keep videos chronicling your early stages in life so that when you grow up and become older, you can always have something to help you remember your childhood. I also aimed for my writing to be a resource and encouragement to other first-time stay-at-home dads. More importantly, I want you to know that the bond and love that we share as father and daughter started well before you were born and has continued to deepen with each passing day.

Journey, understand there are going to come times when you will be upset with me and I will be upset with you. There will be times when you will disappointment me and I will disappointment you. There will also come times when you won't understand that I am not your pal or buddy, but I am your father and my job is to shepherd and guide you through life. My job is also to impress upon you that you are a child of God and you belong to Him first before me.

I want you to know that you are amazing, brilliant, flawed, forgiving, caring, kind, compassionate, fearless, gorgeous, funny, remarkable, sweet, gifted, giving, merciful, intelligent, and lovable. Journey, when you look back and read these words and remember the times shared with Daddy, I want you to feel and know without a shadow of doubt that you are always within the circle of God and Daddy's love. Always! I will never abandon you. You are mine. You are my daughter and I am your daddy and that will never change. Out of all the daughters in the world, God blessed me to be your father. So there is nothing you can ever do that will change that. When life gets hard and you make mistakes, there may be consequences, but that's OK. Come to me first and we will work through it together.

Watching you grow and develop during this first year of your life has been an absolute joy and pleasure. It's a brand new feeling on a daily basis, and Mommy and I are so thankful to God that He brought you into our lives. Just to give you a little heads up and warning, one day you will likely have a little brother or little sister. They will be an entirely different person from you, and Mommy and Daddy will love them the same. You will both require and need different things, and Mommy and Daddy's love is big enough to share.

Happy first birthday, baby girl.

Daddy will always love you.

CPSIA information can be obtained
at www.ICGtesting.com
Printed in the USA
FFOW03n1618050618
47024431-49322FF